Istanbul Diary

ADRIAN KENNY

POOLBEG

Published in 1994 by
Poolbeg,
A division of Poolbeg Enterprises Ltd,
Knocksedan House,
123 Baldoyle Industrial Estate,
Dublin 13, Ireland

A catalogue record for this book is available from the British Library.

ISBN 1 85371 400 3

Cover photograph of *Suleymaniye Mosque, Istanbul*
by K Bossemeyer/Network
Cover design by Poolbeg Group Services Ltd/Red Dog Graphics
Set by Poolbeg Group Services Ltd in Garamond 10/13
Printed by The Guernsey Press Company Ltd,
Vale, Guernsey, Channel Islands.

Biography

Adrian Kenny was born in 1945, studied History at University College Dublin and worked as an English teacher at home and abroad. He is well-known as a freelance journalist and broadcaster. His publications include a novel *The Feast of Michaelmas*, a collection of stories *Arcady*, and an autobiography *Before The Wax Hardened*.

The Publishers gratefully acknowledge the support of

The Arts Council / An Chomhairle Ealaíon.

∽

*"Yashamak bir ağac gibi tek ve hur
Ve bir orman gibi kardeshcesine
Bu hasret bizim!"*
(Nazim Hikmet 1902-63)

(Living is like a tree alone and free
And like a forest friendly
This longing is ours!)

CHAPTER ONE

Istanbul. September 1987

CLICK! THE CRACKLE OF STATIC THEN, AND I'M AWAKE AS THE CALL to prayer explodes from the minaret loudspeaker. For Islam, Edmund tells me, it's day when there's enough light to tell a black thread from a white. Listening to the call spread from mosque to mosque, gathering cock crows and dog barks on the way, I see the sheet stand out slowly from the dark. Then the clock face appears – 6.30. Islam is right, but today is Sunday and I go back to sleep.

Sunday in Istanbul. Not a Christian city – so not a holy day; but a bank holiday – because a European city, although we're on the Asian side and when I open my eyes next I can see out the window the blue blur of hills coming in like waves from Anatolia.

"Six o'clock Greenwich Mean Time," says the calm World Service voice. "A bright morning here in London ... " The sun appears above the apartment block opposite and blazes down full upon me. Gazing back at the shimmering disc, I reflect on the countries it has left behind already. Iraq. Iran. India already slipping into mid-afternoon.

1

Evening – where? Somewhere in the Pacific ... I get out of bed, groping blind in the sudden shadow, putting my T-shirt on back to front, but so eager suddenly to be out in that sun I don't bother to change and in a minute I'm down the grey-veined marble stairs and running slowly along new cement paths between lawns and whirling sprinklers. Other joggers are out already. "Istanbul's muesli belt," Séamus calls it.

Past a blue silk Adidas singlet soaking sweat ... a cigarette jutting from under a black moustache. Good old Turkey! A rush of air and a girl in a Nike track suit lopes ahead, scattering the small fallen gold leaves. Faster, faster down the landscaped slope and across the road, swerving as a cart of gypsy scavengers rattles past. Slower, slower then as the poplar-lined path runs out into baked mud and broken planks and heaps of sand about a new apartment block. End of muesli belt.

Standing there getting my breath back, I hear a sound like huge breathing overhead, and, looking up, I see storks, thousands and white thousands of them high up like cloud, drifting south for the winter. Jogging back slowly up the slope to our *logement* and seeing the familiar white faces appear at the windows, on the balconies, at the door, it strikes me that we're a bit like storks ourselves – English teachers drifting around the world for a living.

I say "Morning" and they say "Morning," all except Séamus, who just nods then glances away, his heavy rimless glasses flashing. He's Irish and freezes up when other Irish are about. A six foot boy, just out of university, querulous de Valera face blushing with pleasure as Gail calls him – "Yo! Séamus, wanna go to the races? There's a meeting in Yenimahalle." She slips an arm through his, linking Grant with her other, and they walk down the road to the bus, Séamus's shrill Galway accent rising above theirs.

There are about two dozen of us living in this concrete wardrobe, each with his own drawer: bedroom, sitting-room-kitchen, bathroom. We meet on the stairs, in the lift; going to collect a glass left behind the night before or passing on old newspapers. The cooking smells drift along the landings, and the different radio stations: World Service, Voice of America, Radio Moscow's English language programme which comes down across the Black Sea clear as a bell in impeccable R.P.

"Had me fooled at first," Geoffrey said, "but then I heard them going on about tractor production, and well, I mean to say ... *you can tell.*"

Geoffrey lives in the flat below mine. His BBC "Lilliburlero" is my back-up alarm clock in the morning. He's elderly, rather lonely. Most evenings after dinner I hear his radio switch off, then his door open and shut and then the scrape of his slippers on the stairs as he comes up to knock on my door. If I don't answer, there's another rustle as he leaves the day before yesterday's *Daily Telegraph* outside and he scrapes off down the stairs and his radio comes on again. When I thank him next day and say, "You should have knocked," he says, "Didn't like to, old boy. Thought you were in bed, which is where I went. Absolutely panned out."

"The old ballocks," Séamus says – he talks to me sometimes, when there's no one about – "Doesn't even say good morning."

Séamus lives across the corridor from Geoffrey. At night I can hear his rock cassettes blaring.

The gypsies, they drift by like the storks. First thing in the morning I see them, scarves about their mouths against the cold, trotting their bony ponies hard, reining up hard when they spot a cardboard box or a cement bag. Sometimes they go too far, go into the building sites and then the watchman appears and starts shouting at them and they run back to their carts. They could drive all day and still be in these tower block suburbs.

Istanbul: it means simply Into the City. City of crowds pouring down these concrete canyons as if to an immense football match, city of standing-room only. On the ferry boat today, wedged against a shaven-headed private soldier. He scratched, bent back a brown flap ear and Sultan Ahmet appeared, St Sophia, Topkapi on its acropolis cliff – all vanishing as the ear snapped back into place like a shutter.

A bit of our neighbourhood hasn't been built up yet. I went for a walk there the other evening. It must have been a village once: you could see some crossroad cottages and a piece of the old road with brambles growing through a stone wall. I climbed over, not knowing what the notice *"Dikkat! Köpek Var"* meant, and walked across a flowery meadow and a stream to have a look at an old Ottoman timber mansion, all boarded up, a JCB parked outside the door. Then up out of the meadow grass all around me dogs' heads appeared, huge mongrel Alsatians. I was so frightened I couldn't move. People passing by along the road stopped to watch. There was quite a crowd before I made a move, when the dogs moved too, snarling quietly. I got to a weeping willow tree where I broke off a branch. It made a noise like a rifle shot and the dogs turned and ran. *"Alman?"* a Turk said to me as I climbed trembling out over the wall. The Germans here have a name for being recklessly adventurous.

Edmund tells me the gypsies live up near Edirne Kapi. I met him at Mass – Armenian – last Sunday and we went for coffee afterwards. He's bought a German *Baedeker* – he loves Germany as only a disaffected Englishman can – and translated the passage about the gypsy quarter, lingering over the last sentence: "Not a place for those easily shocked."

"I got a taxi up there right away, but *I* couldn't see anything. A few gypsy girls dancing in the streets, that's all. Of course it was only five o'clock in the evening. Could be different at night *time*."

He has a deep, educated Liverpool accent, very much his own, which throws the emphasis onto unexpected words.

"Lovely creatures, though. There was *one* – she couldn't have been more than sixteen, a real beauty. Scarlet pyjama trousers, dusty brown feet, beautiful *toes*. And her face – it was shaded by her scarf but I went up to ask directions – you know, a fine straight nose, an aristocratic-looking girl. But *she* wasn't interested ... "

When I met Edmund first, I thought he was dying. He's about sixty, with a ghastly yellow face and old National Health glasses. He uses a Ventolin inhaler. Now that I've got to know him better, I see that he's as tough as wire. When he puts the Ventolin in his pocket, he takes out his cigarettes. "Did *you* see that girl at Mass? In the choir?"

"The dark one?"

"I think she smiled at me. Mmm – I'm afraid she's given me the old *itch*. If I'm not careful, I shall be down in the *kips* this afternoon."

The waiter arrived with our order. He'd misunderstood my pidgin Turkish and, instead of pastries, brought two cooked sheep's eyes, a poor man's delicacy here. Edmund glanced down at the cold blue orbs gazing up at him from the plate and almost retched.

"Bloody barbarians!" He led the way out into the street, stepping back almost as suddenly when he saw Geoffrey go by – dark suit, striped tie, Common Prayer book clasped behind back.

"He's all right," I said, though I stepped back too.

"I run a *mile* from people like that in England."

Besides people like Geoffrey, the only other type Edmund seems to dislike is the male homosexual. He likes Jews, Arabs, Blacks, Irish. His best friend in England is lesbian, he tells me.

"A funny *thing* – I've never yet liked a queer." Another whiff of the Ventolin – he breathes it in with the same sort of relish he inhales the incense at Mass – and he walked alongside me in a springy lope down to the ferry. We had decided to go to a party Norbert was giving.

"In fact, I can't even stand a bloke with a moustache because of that. The first *bloke* ever to try it on with me, he had a moustache. Do you *know* Liverpool?"

"To pass through."

"I haven't been back for twenty years. But I was on *this* tram – I was about twelve – and this bloke with a moustache sat down beside me, *upstairs*. Next thing, he put his hand on my balls. I pressed the *bell* and he got such a bloody fright, he ran down the stairs and jumped off. The bloody tram was doing about thirty miles an hour. He must have broken every bone in his body!" He has a great schoolboy laugh.

"Norbert hasn't a moustache."

"He hasn't even got hair. Do you know, that's a toupee he wears. A priest with a toupee – it's a bit *fishy,* isn't it?"

Norbert is "The Co-ordinator for Foreign Teachers." He's a great one for titles. I called him "Norbert" recently and got a very sharp put-down. "Dr Norbert C. Hopkins, BEd, MA, Dip TEFL, Cert Ed." is the heading on the memos that appear on our wardrobe noticeboard. We call him "Dr Norbert". Séamus called him "Father" once, but he held out his hands in an Urbi et Orbi of horror and cried *"Please!"*.

He's a Catholic priest, we think. He lives on a suburban island in the Sea of Marmara.

The smell from Marmara is terrible. Going along the coast road home from work in the evenings, car drivers roll up their windows. It's raw sewage locked in oil discharge and industrial waste. The sea still looks beautiful, like a sheet of sky blue glass, with pretty camp sites along the European shore where Polish and Yugoslav families come in summer. I suppose Turkey's the only place where their currency is worth anything. When there's a shore breeze blowing, they let down the tent flaps and lace them shut. Last year a tanker blew up in the bay – there's a pyramid of fused iron jutting up from the water still – and some crewmen were killed. The bodies were never recovered, so for months afterwards there was a ban on selling fish caught hereabouts.

I mentioned that to Edmund as he bought a fish sandwich from one of the boatmen along the quay. They fry them in braziers in the bilges.

"At my age it doesn't really matter." He gazed absently across the Golden Horn's blue green slick, up at the Galata Hill. "Do *you* see that red neon sign, the Kodak advertisement? That's my landmark for the kips. Just to the right of that. Mmm – " he bit into the fried fish, saying with his mouth full " – all I can think of is *cunt.*"

I thought at first my typewriting might disturb Geoffrey, but when I asked him he said, "Don't hear a thing, laddie. You carry on. Bit of a writer, are you?"

"I'm keeping a diary," I said, which was true. At first, every evening, I typed out a page of things I had seen or heard during the day. But after a few weeks, looking at the thickening folder and thinking of previous diaries I kept, never read and finally threw out, I threw it out too (except these few pages – I can never quite do anything thoroughly).

The gypsies took it. I saw them this morning making off at a run as the porter appeared, throwing amongst other things into their cart my pages describing them, rattling on then to the next concrete wardrobe.

CHAPTER TWO

THE SIMPLEST WAY TO GET WORK VISAS WAS TO CROSS INTO Greece, to the Turkish consulate in Komotini just over the border. There were so many of us – English, Irish, American, Australian and all the others whose native tongue happens to be a market commodity – that Dr Norbert hired a coach, a glossy Mercedes which attracted lots of attention in our street.

It was October, the evening getting cool, but the locals were still strolling up and down arm in arm, men with men, women with women, all chewing sunflower seeds, holding onto summer. When Dr Norbert himself appeared – brown leather shorts, Peanuts T-shirt, fat leather handbag dangling from wrist – all eyes turned from the coach.

"Quite frankly," Geoffrey murmured, "I think the man's a disgrace to his cloth." He looked up smartly though when Dr Norbert called his name and beckoned him on board. There was something not to be argued with in Norbert, even – in fact all the more so – when he wore his outrageous clothes. Standing up on the coach steps with clipboard and biro, he called us one by one, checked that we had our passports and then directed us down the coach, calling after me, flapping his hand when I tried to sit at the back. "No, let's try to keep it tight for the time being, Adrian. Yes, there, beside Tom." He was good at remembering names.

Tom had hardly spoken to me since I arrived. The thought of an eight-hour journey beside him made me blank. I suppose it showed. He drawled "Hello" in the nasal accent he put on, then he looked out the window. He had a pale, drinker's face. He had never been drinking with me though; just as Edmund kept away from Geoffrey, Tom kept away from Séamus, me and the other Irish. Now I think about it, everyone kept away from their own kind except the Americans, who stuck together like midges.

It was dark by the time we set off, Dr Norbert standing facing us, switching on a courier's microphone as the Mercedes swung down onto the Western highway. He liked being on stage.

"Friends – '*arkadashlar*,' as I am sure you are saying by now – welcome, '*hoshgeldinis!*' I think you will agree that as of now we are on a little 'freebie'. Yes, our trip to Greece is necessary. We must go. We must get our work permits. We must return. But we will enjoy ourselves, we will 'cross the border,' we will be 'abroad.' Our 'ETA' is ... "

"Mother o'Jazes," Tom said in mock Irish, the start of a conversation, I thought, but he cancelled it by taking a book from his blazer pocked and reading. *The Art of Loving* by Erich Fromm, I noticed as he lit a cigarette. He inhaled completely, clamping his long white fingers across his mouth.

The lines of apartment blocks went by, so exactly the same they gave the impression we were standing still, looking at a single scene: a boy sitting on an autocycle talking with another boy; two old men sitting side by side on chairs; above, a girl chin on hand looking out a window – wide open showing the interior ... glaring overhead light,

10

fat, head-scarved woman in flowery pyjama trousers sitting cross-legged on the carpet making white lace, looking up now and then at a huge colour tv. Behind and behind and behind, the lights of other apartment blocks receded up the hill into a single sheet of light.

"Fucking useless light." Tom put up a hand and pressed buttons overhead. One put out the tiny light there was, another brought a rush of cold air. He put down his book, pressed the button that let back the seat, and the yellow hiking boots he wore rose into sight.

And still the tower blocks, mile after mile. They say seven hundred people arrive in Istanbul every day, in from Anatolia. Whenever I was up about Edirne Kapi, I saw them coming from the bus station with their tablecloth bundles. Tom's book slipped off his lap and I picked it up and put it back on again. He pressed the seat button and sat forward, yawning. He looked out the window at the apartment lights, going out now one by one.

"'The unpurged images of day recede; the Emperor's drunken soldiery are abed' – hah?"

"Who's that?" I said. "Yeats?"

"Ten out of ten." The accent was coming down slowly. We circled each other warily.

"'Byzantium?'"

"We did it for the Leaving."

I wasn't sure if he was being serious or not. Not, I decided, as he added, "1968" – pause – "AD."

The apartment blocks thinned away, reappeared, then disappeared finally and we were flying along a flat highway between fields of ripe sunflowers lit by moonlight. *"Aychichek*, they call them in Turkish," I remarked, " – moonflowers."

"Everything's back to front here."

"You don't like it?"

"It's a job."

11

"Good land," I said.

He looked out the window at the huge rich fields. "Haven't we as good at home" – mock Irish again.

"Do you go back much?"

"Not a lot," Tom said and I caught his natural voice, middle-class nondescript as my own. It was like a cautious handshake and we lay back into our seats, into our own thoughts.

What was I doing there? Teaching English. But why in Istanbul, when I had a wife and children in Ireland? Because I couldn't get a job anywhere else. My CV, at first sight a convincing story, to close study was a story of decline: from the first foothold in university teaching, down into secondary school, National School subbing, private tuition, TEFL. There was a reason for it, naturally – I had spent my time trying to write. But a writer is no more different from a reader than a shopkeeper from a customer. Everyone has a reason for ending up as an English language teacher, at least in an outfit like Dr Norbert's. "Like the Australian army," Geoffrey used to say. " – two balls and an arsehole and you're in." He wasn't saying that now, I thought. Sitting beside Norbert, running a finger inside his tight blue-striped collar, he listened and nodded respectfully, as glad as the rest of us to have a job.

The air brakes sighed as the driver slowed and swung into a service station and the dead straight road ahead vanished. The Roman legions who made it must have stopped at posts as remote, heard the same noises, cicadas and frogs, treble and alto, calling from the darkness all around. It was cold now, but the same boy was sitting on the same autocycle chatting with another boy, and the old men were still sitting out on chairs, turning from their worry beads to watch the foreigners climbing down from the coach.

"Is this – " Dr Norbert peeped around the restaurant door: colour tv playing swooning Turkish music, farm labourers mopping up bean stew with bread, " – a safe place for a white man?" He led the way to the counter, unzipped the maroon leather handbag. "The Milky Bars are on me!"

"Time for a beer, have we?"

"A beer? I'm sure you have, Tom. One beer, please. Oh God, he doesn't understand. *Bir bira, lutfen. Bira. Evet ...* and Edmund?"

"Tea'll do me."

"Please!" Dr Norbert raised hands to his hazel toupee. "Not tea! Have you not seen how they make it?"

"I like the *stuff.*"

"Be it on your own ... stomach. *Bir chay.* Oooh, can't bear to look." He turned away as the thimble of boiling tar was dropped into a glass, topped up then with hot water. "How much? Two hundred liras. Edmund, you are forever in my debt. And Irene? Yes indeed, I am paying ... "

I moved away, chatting with Tom, but the connection had been made. The farm workers turned, staring at us.

"Wonder where we are?"

"God knows. Still in Turkey."

"Next stop, the promised land." Edmund joined us. "I've just been looking in my *Baedeker.* Do you know, the border with Greece is the River Maritsa. That was the River Hebron. You know, where the Maenads threw Orpheus."

Edmund was a Latin teacher until the grammar schools folded up. He talked about the classical past as if it was last week.

"Really?" Tom had his posh drawl again. He let down a quarter litre of beer in one swallow.

"Or his head, rather. *Horace* says the mouth went on singing as it floated down to the sea."

"I hear the exchange rate is terrible." Irene approached

with a pastry and a bottle of Coke. "Unless you've dollars or sterling."

As Geoffrey too drifted over, we turned and saw Dr Norbert standing alone at the counter.

"Have I 'BO'?" the David Hockney voice cried across the heads of the farm workers. "Is there something my closest friends won't tell me?" He sniffed under his arm. The farm workers laughed suddenly all together and there was a moment's awkward silence. Then Norbert, all five foot two of him, shimmied over to their table and sat on its edge, crossed his bare white plump legs with a coquette's flourish. "Here I am welcome. Here I have true friends. Here – " he reached over a hurdle of sunburnt arms and took a bottle of water, flicked off the tinfoil cap and drank, " – is purity!"

"*Aferin!*" they cried. "Bravo!"

"Might as well have another." Tom strolled over to the counter with his empty bottle.

A bray of the horn, a flash of full headlamps that lit up a straight kilometre ahead and the coach pulled out into the road. Dr Norbert stood up and click! microphone in hand took the stage again.

"Fellow pilgrims! It is the midnight hour. It is time for sleep. Those of you feeling cold will find in the rack overhead ... a blanket. We shall switch out the light. We shall press the button that tilts back the seat. We shall leave Turkey to the frogs, the cicadas and the owls. Geoffrey – a red-blooded male with a wife, albeit in England – and I shall sleep side by side. Those of you with no such, shall I say, faith, will find vacant seats at the back of the coach. Sweet dreams! *Iyi geceler!*"

Laughter and applause.

"Talk about sermons," Tom muttered in the dark. "Wouldn't you know he's a priest."

"Hard to believe."

14

"He was dressed as one when he interviewed me. I suppose it helps in Ireland."

"Go back home between jobs, do you?"

"I was back for a funeral. My father died."

"Sorry," I said. I felt his shoulders shrug in the dark. He pressed back his seat and in a minute he was breathing hoarsely.

No lights outside either. The flat farmland of Thrace was asleep. Only the tunnel of our headlamps down which we were speeding. The power of that Mercedes engine. Each touch on the accelerator carried us along still faster, silently like a sea wave.

I woke with a start – from a nightmare, I thought until I felt my head bang on the chrome back of the seat in front. Then I saw others falling out of their seats. Someone screamed. There was a scraping sound as if a tin can was caught under the coach and was being dragged along the road. Then we left the road and the coach plunged over rough ground. A telegraph pole appeared by my window and we stopped. Back across the road I could see a service station like the one we had left – when? hours ago, by the taste in my mouth. I looked at my watch – two-thirty, looked out the window and saw a smashed-up car on the road. Our driver seemed all right. He was trying to open the coach door. The dashboard button didn't work, but the emergency handle did and we got out in a crowd, shivering in the cold.

There was steam pouring from the car engine which was crushed up into the chassis. By the light of the service station, from which people were coming at a run, we could see a young man in the driver's seat. The windscreen was smashed open but the dashboard was buckled up about him like a belt so the men dragged open a door and drew him out that way. His legs were caught under the steering-shaft; they tugged, he made a bubbling sound like a drowning kitten, then his legs came free and they laid him on the road. Someone got a blanket from the coach and he was rolled onto that and they straightened him, which was easy: every bone in his body seemed to have been broken. He made a snuffling sound and then lay still. He looked to have been in his early twenties. We stood around in silence looking at the blood soaking into the blanket, looking at each other – faces clay-white in the sodium glare. From behind a line of poplar trees, above the rattle of their leaves, came the hollow rattle of sheep bells; then a shepherd appeared in a huge felt cloak with a pointed hood, leaning on his staff to stare. Eerily, the car radio was still playing.

"Got ya!" Dr Norbert slapped his white thigh and lifted a hand to show the mosquito he had killed.

CHAPTER THREE

17 October 1987

COAL DELIVERY FOR THE WINTER: TWENTY LUMPS, EACH WEIGHING A ton, spilled in one thunder-roar from the lorry. Our street is strewn with these megalithic tombs.

Diary writing again. Kerem, a huge-headed scholarship boy, made me a present of this notebook. So far, I've been given a thousand cigarettes, two bottles of wine, a vest, a bottle of Scotch and a handkerchief. Like the others, Kerem feels this has established special-relationship status. Today he slipped me a photo of himself and his mother; on the back he had written, "I, Kerem and my mother. My father is dead, passed away, died with his boots on."

The English dictionary is everywhere; not just in school. Everyone seems to have one in his pocket with his identity papers.

In class the children lean towards me from their desks, as if they're on the wrong side of a ravine and I'm on the other with a rope.

The English language is a million pound industry. The

Oxford University Press rep. (gel hair, Guildford Cricket Club tie) was in school the other day and took an order for a hundred copies of some cartoon-strip textbook.

OUP rep. – "We call it the 'play way' of learning English."

Headmaster (retired army officer, face like Nero) nodding gravely – "The play way ... "

In class this morning: "What's the plural of 'mouse'?"

Cem, stepping back, then quickly forward as if about to jump across the ravine: "Micky."

The class laughed and turned around to look at Cem, screwing up their eyes as if he was far away, turning to me again breathing the word across to me, toes flexing, ready to spring up and proclaim it. Cem, eyes goggling, hissing for help in Turkish, no one turning back to help him. I turned to Çigdem, a front row beauty, and she shot up shouting, "Mice!", rocking on the balls of her feet, ready for more. "Another, teacher, please."

"Blouse?"

"Blice!"

The class laughed as one, Cem bending forwards to hold his sides. Çigdem spun around and shouted something in Turkish, whirled back to face me, pleading, "Another, teacher. *Please.*"

She spent the rest of class sobbing face-down on her desk.

21 October 1987

A lone, last, lost stork circling high above the tower blocks, around and around and around.

From up there, as from the plane that brought me here, Istanbul is a child's jigsaw of a few big pieces: the Black Sea, the Bosphorous strait cutting down to the Sea of

Marmara; on one side the Asiatic city, on the other the European – in turn divided by the waters of the Golden Horn. Yet, down here, I felt helpless as a child, only now getting together this sea-land-bridge-crossing city.

In Kadiköy – once Chalcedon – this evening, doing what I like best: nothing, lounging against an old Greek Orthodox church watching a JCB cut away the slope below to widen the street. Work stopped suddenly and the driver got down from his cabin and called the other men over. In the usual instinctive way there was a crowd about in thirty seconds. We watched as a man with a shovel scraped away thick yellow clay, then saw what the JCB had struck, and smashed – the stone lid of a sarcophagus. It seems to be a regular thing here: the foreman sauntered off down the street – to report it, I suppose. The lid, incised with a Byzantine cross, had been smashed open, so we all leaned forward to look inside.

"*Yok.*" An old man clicked his tongue against the roof of his mouth and tilted back his head. And there was, literally, nothing. It was spotlessly empty as the day it had been made.

27 October 1987

Thirty years ago I was a compulsive wanker. Now I'm a compulsive scribbler. It helps me to sleep, jotting the day's scraps which otherwise go around in my head at night.

On the European side today, I dropped into a tourist bar for a drink. At the next table an Irish woman was being chatted up by a Turkish student. He went to buy another round, her eye caught mine and we began to speak. An almost audible clang as the Irish country defence system fell into place. Through the portcullis we exchanged pleasantries. I was from Dublin; she was from Westmeath. She didn't like Dublin, if she was going to live in a city she would rather live in a real one, not some provincial hole etc. The student returned with her gin and tonic, she drank it speedily and left. The Turkish student sighed like a ham actor, then joined me.

He spoke perfect English with an American accent. He has a university scholarship: the government gives him seventeen dollars a month – "I know, it is terrible." He had spent it in this bar over the past few days. He used to stay in a student hostel, but after the last political troubles the police closed it down. Now he stays with relations – a four-bus, two-hour journey away from the college. He had been picked up by police after the troubles – "To frighten me." They took him down to the station, then downstairs to the –

Mortified at not knowing the word, he took out his dictionary and flew through the worn-black pages – "Torture. To the torture room." On the wall they had written THERE IS NO ALLAH. That was because when men were tortured they cried out to God. Suddenly he began to cry, the tears shining his drink-reddened nose.

1 November 1987

Tom's been transferred to the school I teach in. "A punishment posting," Geoffrey calls it. It wasn't until he joined us that I realised most of the Irish teachers are in the same school, the poorest and most remote in the organisation. "Oh yes," Irene sniffed when I remarked on it, "anything will do for us." In fact, I was appointed to a school in a rich suburb of white apartment houses but asked for a transfer to the European side: I liked the idea of a morning drive across the Bosphorous. "My heart *bleeds* for you," Dr Norbert sighed as he agreed. I saw what he meant when, after a seventy-minute minibus drive, I arrived. The school is between a shanty town and a prison on the open road to Bulgaria.

Drink landed Tom here, a three-day bender. He went on the wagon straight away – although he still sleeps it out in the mornings, cold and dark and misty now. I had to go up and knock on his door again today. When he answered, I couldn't help noticing over his shoulder in the bedroom Stephanie, the best-looking girl in the place. When he appeared five minutes later, buttoning his navy blazer, he sat down beside me at the back of the minibus without the trace of a smile.

"I think that's everyone," Irene says always as she climbs in, shutting the door after her and pulling her blue woolly hat down over her ears.

"*Tamam?*" Ali revved the engine. "OK?"

"Songul?" one of the Turkish teachers said. They take a lift from us.

"Look!" Séamus flared. "We said a quarter past."

Another Turkish teacher looked at his watch. "It is ten past." They murmured in Turkish together and Séamus murmured, "*Póg mo thóin.*" Ali got out and polished his windscreen until Songul appeared, coming down the broken frozen muddy street at a run.

"*Tamam?*"

"Tam bloody am."

The minibus set off. Apologising, explaining, saying good morning all at once, Songul sat down. "My clock, it stopped! And I did not wake up until half-past five o'clock ... "

"And what time do you usually get up, Songul?"

"The time I usually get up, Tom, is half-past four o'clock. To do my school preparations I must to get up at this time." She smiled and took out her cigarettes, putting them away quickly as Séamus flared again – "No smoking in the bus!"

"Pardon! Pardon! I forget. You are right, Sea-mouse. It is a good rule – no smoking in the bus. Turkish people, they

21

smoke too much. Turkish people ... " The other Turkish teachers looked away. Songul makes them cringe in the same way Séamus makes Tom cringe.

"Did you hear your man this morning – the muezzin? Talk about the fucking Angelus ... " As Séamus started gabbling, Tom turned and looked out the window at the mist and the mud and the workmen slogging across the building sites, shovels on shoulders. Where the old Ottoman timber mansion stood a few months ago, there's a foundation pit for another tower block, half full of rain already. Along its cliff edge half-a-dozen filthy scrawny brown sheep grazed, watched by a boy wearing a Walkman. We shot through the old village crossroads, throwing a brown sheet of water across a bus queue. Ali waved a fist at them and turned on his wipers, putting his foot down as he hit the *asfalti*, racing all the other minibuses for a few kilometres and then we met the motorway. The traffic snaked into lane, slowed, made a convulsive start and then stopped dead.

"Allahallah ... " Ali got out, talking to himself and shining his windscreen. Through it we saw half a mile of other drivers doing the same.

"What's he saying, Songul?"

"He is saying, Irene, that we must begin more early," Songul smiled. She looks like Alice in Wonderland. "Tomorrow I will get up at four o'clock!"

This is the time, as Ali moves in furious little spurts towards the Bosphorous bridge, that Irene takes out her *Irish Independent*, spreads it on her knees and irons out the fold marks, then folds it in half. Each morning Tom stares at her as closely as she looks at the paper, his lips moving faintly sometimes as if identifying each part of her dress: grey pixie boots ... teak-coloured tights; his face completely expressionless, even when Irene reads bits out to us – "And Charlie Haughey's daughter got married. Hmm!"

The only time she looks up is when we cross the bridge, when the dammed-up traffic finally gets through the toll-gates and floods flat-out across the Bosphorous. "I love that view up to the Black Sea," she murmurs, and Tom's gaze follows hers through the pall of exhaust gas and the tangle of suspension cables up the grey misty waters. She goes back to the *Irish Independent* as soon as we reach the other side.

"Breakfast in Asia, lunch in Europe," Tom says.

"Had you time for breakfast?" I thought I'd gone too far. The expressionless gaze turned on me.

"Better not let on." He has the Irish knack of talking naturally under his breath. "She's engaged."

"Not to you?"

"He's in England."

"What's she doing out here?"

"He's studying for his finals. Medicine or something. Steph said she'd get out of the way till he finished."

"She's nice."

"Never noticed her till the other day. I was hanging around Kadiköy, having a cup of coffee. I laid off the beer. And she was at the next table. We just hit it off." He took out his cigarettes, stopped and put them back in his pocket. "What do you make of your man Sea-mouse?"

"He's very young."

"He's that all right."

"Hey, listen to this ... " While Irene reads the newspaper on the way to school, Séamus reads history, big books on Byzantium. Like her, he reads pieces aloud to us. His voice shrills as if he can't keep what he's read to himself. " ... by 1180 AD there were 60,000 Westerners in Constantinople ... "

"All teaching English," Tom muttered.

"Right!" Séamus's cockatoo laugh filled the bus and even Songul smiled.

In a way I have to admire Séamus's general *Je m'en fouterie.*
During our free periods, when everyone else in the
staffroom is sitting around the table marking exercise
books, Séamus is lying on the couch, feet up, reading about
Byzantium. A touchy topic for most Turks, and I could see
why when I looked at his latest book, something by
Runciman, an old Cambridge hand. After reading a page of
imitation Augustan prose on the fall of Constantinople in
1453 (the irrevocable descent into darkness, barbarism and
dirt, etc.), I went back to marking homework.

This phil-Hellene strand is as much a part of English
culture as cricket, but I was surprised when Edmund, a true
cricket hater, turned out to be anti-Turk too. "Like a
Victorian public lavatory" was his comment on some Iznik
tile work I admired in a mosque one day. The mosques, he
claims, are mechanical variations of St Sophia. There's a half
truth there, but if you are looking for a line of descent from
classical Greece, the pedigree which comes from Athenian
temple to Byzantine church to Turkish mosque seems no
less flawed than that descending via Rome, Romanesque
and Gothic; while the baths, the very centre of ancient
social life, vanished from the West now, are alive in the
Turkish *hamam.* Anyway, the Turks take a firm line with
what's left of their Greek population, rub it in a bit too hard
indeed. For example, every Greek Orthodox church has to
fly the star and crescent flag. "Suits me," Edmund says.
"*Makes* them easier to find."

Ventolin in one hand, *Baedeker* in the other, he spends
his free day combing the back streets for Byzantine beauties.

I have to take back what I said about Runciman. (After forty we spend half our time taking back what we said.) Séamus fell asleep on the bus home this evening and I read some more of his book.

"The complacency of Hellenic naturalism was meaningless to them. Nature to them was often ugly and they were prepared to face its ugliness. They dispensed with delicacy of drawing and balance of composition; they required an art that would speak directly to them without compromise, that would rouse them to intensity of emotion rather than lull them into an aesthetic content."

I learned also: "The servant girl who spat accidentally out of an upper window onto the coffin of the Empress Eudoxia (412 AD) was put to death on the very tomb."

And: "A statue of Aphrodite marked the only brothel in the city in the quarter called Zeugma on the Golden Horn."

And: "Corn was the same price in Constantinople in 906 AD as in 1914."

15 November 1987

I had never realised just how much cricket is played around the world. Like death, I suppose, it's always happening somewhere and Geoffrey manages to pick it up on his radio. In one way I don't mind. I spend my evenings writing: it's a novel about when I was young, and the forgotten jargon drifting up from Geoffrey's flat brings back those days which are suddenly becoming remote. Why does youth fall into place in middle age? Because we have finished living? Or at last begun to live? These are the times, when I try to compose large final thoughts, that the endless commentary becomes a bloody nuisance.

" ... Runs up ... off-break again ... just a shade short and Botham – oh my word! Botham really getting behind that one, and Alan Border is shaking his head. Not a nice feeling being hit for ... yes, it's a six, it's a six, another six for Ian Botham ... "

So when there was a knock on my door around nine o'clock and Tom asked me out for a drink, I didn't need persuading.

"There's a place down in Bostanci isn't bad," he said. We went downstairs, out into the freezing November dark.

"How's Stephanie?"

"Tell you about that." He waved down a taxi and in five minutes we were dropped outside a seaside bar.

"Hi-lo, Tom!" The owner knew his name, so did a few other men standing against high, narrow tables. The place smelled of raki, frying lamb chops and Turkish tobacco. There was a Kung Fu film – English subtitles, Turkish dubbing – going full blast on the tv.

"*Tá go maith agus níl go holc.*" Tom led the way to a table by the stove. "Beer OK?" He called over to the bar. "Ahmed! *Iki bira, lutfen!*"

"You're off the wagon?"

"For the weekend. Steph and I thought we'd head off to Thermal in the morning. Have you been there? Lovely old Turkish baths there."

"Where is she tonight?"

"With her fiancé. He came out the other day."

The beer arrived. Tom has the knack of just opening his throat; his Adam's apple doesn't move, the beer just flows down. "Good old beer, Efes. That's the Turkish for Ephesus. Steph wanted to go down there, but it's a bit far for a weekend."

"But what brought her fiancé out?"

"She's a nice girl, Steph. Dead straight. She wrote to your man and told him – you know, how she'd met me."

"What's he like?"

"Didn't meet him. I didn't want to. Anyway, they've been knocking around together the last couple of days. She likes him. Naturally."

26

"And she likes you too."

"This is it. This is it. She suggested some sort of half shares relationship, but I said I wasn't interested in that sort of stuff – you know, that she'd have to make her mind up. So – " he finished the beer in another swallow " – she's giving him the bullet this evening."

"Phew!"

"I think she's glad to be out of it. She's very young. Only twenty-two." He glanced up at the tv. "Good old Bruce Lee."

Tom must be nearly forty.

18 November 1987

Stormy night. Too rough for Dr Norbert to sail back to his island, so he's staying here (it seems he has a drawer in this wardrobe), strolling the corridors, paying calls, like a parish priest except for his clothes: bright pink T-shirt, with the motto WINE ME DINE ME SIXTY-NINE ME rucked up on his small paunch.

Geoffrey: "I say, do you suppose he's a ... you know, a bum-puncher?"

An owl called outside my window all night.

19 November 1987

I dropped down to Geoffrey again tonight. It's like walking into an English sitting-room. Richard Baker on the World Service, *Financial Times* on the couch. No mantelpiece, so the invitations are standing on the window ledge: C of E tea, British Council lecture. The invitation to a British Consulate reception – gild-edged, copperplate, red embossed lion and unicorn – is too important for the window ledge. It stands on the table propped against a volume of Anthony Powell, Geoffrey's favourite novelist. He talks about and quotes Powell's characters as if he was at school with them – maybe he was.

"While the rose blows along the river brink With old String-ham the ruby vintage drink," he says as I appear with my bottle and glass. "Take a pew, old boy. I'll brew up some Riza chay."

"Try some wine, it's better than their tea."

"That wouldn't be hard. No – leave the stuff alone now. Got to the stage I wanted brandy for breakfast, I said, 'Row for shore, Geoffrey'."

He potters about the kitchenette, humming along to Richard Baker's next record.

21 November 1987

The mud, inches of it on the streets and paths like grey glue. The old people accept it, crawling along with grey goloshes of it on their shoes, stopping now and then to kick some off against a wall or stand in a puddle to dissolve it. In the shanty town beside our school the paths between the tiny cottages are like flooded ploughland. Each table-sized garden is crammed with village symbols of prosperity: beehive, fig tree, goat. I went for a walk there after lunch (Migros supermarket bags over my shoes) and ran into a wedding. A girl was being married from a shack fifty yards of whipped mud away from the road. A taxi arrived blaring its horn, then the groom in a waxed and polished banger and then a minibus full of guests – Anatolian women, gold teeth flashing as they u-lu-lued, henna-stained hands waving tea towels out the windows. The shack door opened and the family appeared, followed by the bride, a girl in grown-up, dazzling white clothes, her forehead strung with gold coins. She looked across the lake of mud to where her groom was standing and then suddenly broke away from her family, who were about to carry her, and ran like a wagtail across the grey surface. Somehow the mud's skin didn't break and she reached the taxi with hardly a spot on her white satin slippers.

Beyond the shanty town the land slopes up into ridges, utterly bare. Even the gypsies have stopped coming up here to scavenge. Even the heather they were pulling up to make into besoms is gone. The goats are eating the roots, their teeth smeared with clay. The view from the top is desolate, except for soldiers patrolling a mile of barbed wire fence. All this heathland – bronze heather, furze and scrub birch – belongs to an army barracks and in the middle of it is Turkey's maximum security prison. It's called Metris.

23 November 1987

Letter from John in Dubai: "Lying by the pool drinking iced wine and watching the air hostesses jumping in and out ... "

Serdar Bey, our vice-principal, spends his free time making a relief model of Constantinople under siege by Sultan Mehmet Fatih. It takes up a full-sized table-tennis table and includes every detail. The Byzantines' chain across the mouth of the Golden Horn is a real chain. A line of model ships sails along the blue plaster sea by the Marmara walls to where dozens of toy turbaned soldiers are waiting to tow the fleet on rollers overland to the Horn inside the chain. He has the city walls lined with more toy soldiers, their faces painted white to show they are terrified Christians. He can't wait to use the tube of red paint, squeezing a drop onto his fingertip with which he pushes a defending soldier down off the rampart –
    "Poh!"

Because of the mud, the traffic is so bad that Ali takes a different road these days, cutting through the army land between the barracks and the prison: a shocking road with bath-sized potholes, deliberately kept in disrepair; I suppose to discourage anyone mad enough to try a hit and run rescue. Every morning we see new recruits arriving for their eighteen months' national service: miserable-looking teenagers in jeans and trainers with imitation Adidas shoulder bags. If they're at the barracks gate as we pass, Ali slows down to call out encouragement. Then he turns to us and mimes their reception, swiping his hand back and forth (the sergeant slapping them across the face), then snip-snipping with his fingers (their hair being shaved off). Sometimes he mimes the future of the prisoners these soldiers guard: clamping fingers and thumb about his neck, jerking his head upwards, then letting it fall limp sideways onto his shoulders.

It seems the prison was built after the 1980 troubles, when the army stepped in, but the trials are still going on. The new screening trees, groves of poplars with white-washed trunks, are not tall enough yet to conceal the building – a windowless cement bunker surrounded by barbed wire fences, searchlights, towers with machine guns. Beyond that is a moat. My Turkish is good enough now to understand Ali's chant as we pass by: "Not even a bird could escape from there!"

Other days, when a lorry slips into a pothole and the prison road is blocked, we go by a back road. This circles the army land and we see lines of soldiers out on patrol lugging heavy rifles, their great coats sodden from the waist-high heather. Sometimes they put up a snipe and pretend to shoot. From the classroom I can hear the new intake drilling, a warm dull roar as they chant to the thunder of a drum.

Naturally, when Dr Norbert visits us he comes by taxi. He arrived this week to inspect the new teachers, looking like an ambassador – one of those tiny Eastern diplomats you see only in newspaper photos: the wig like a hard hat, a pale lightweight suit, silk tie, soft black leather shoes.

"What about the others?" Séamus flared when he heard that he was first on the list. "Irene? Adrian? Tom? Are you inspecting them too?"

"True, Séamus, true." Squeeze on elbow. "However, Irene is an experienced National School teacher. And Adrian ... " He took my CV from his folder, a sharp glance taking the tissue off the flimsy bones below; that, or simply to keep Séamus happy, decided him to inspect me too.

"Stuff you, ducky," he murmured as Séamus bounded off. He was back in his fruity voice when he appeared at my classroom door later on. "Carry on, Mr Kenny." He sat at the rostrum table, took out a notebook, nodding gravely as I gabbled a few old TEFL phrases: Conversational Structures ... Building on Basic Modules. I had Kerem stand up and asked him his name.

"My name is Kerem Urtugay."

"Kerem, how old are you?"

"I am fourteen years old."

Dr Norbert unscrewed a fountain pen. The class gazed at him across the ravine, glared at Kerem, waving their hands hysterically as I asked him even more questions.

"Why do you want to learn English?"

"Because it is an international language."

"Why do you want to learn an international language?" The shanty town children swung-hung on the railings, waving at me through the windows upside down.

"Because I want to be a brain surgeon."

31

"When you are a brain surgeon, where will you work?"

"First I will go to London and New York. But then I will return to the Turkey." Colossal sniggers from the rest of the class.

"Why will you return to Turkey?" The school porter appeared in the yard with a fistful of stones.

"Because it is my Mother Country." Kerem gave his olive oil smile.

"Thank you, Kerem."

"Excuse me, teacher – this mark goes into my report?"

The class hushed for an answer, but did not get it. Dr Norbert stood up, screwed the cap back on his pen. "That's quite satisfactory. One suggestion – try to get the others involved, even in a 'one-to-one' situation." He shut the notebook. I noticed the cover as he slipped it into his pocket: Chelsea Building Society.

"That's Norbert," Gail said when I mentioned it to her, " – he likes showing off."

27 November 1987

One of Songul's many jobs is writing out sayings of Ataturk on sheets of cartridge paper for Serdar Bey. The door opens, the powerful black moustached face appears and calls indiscriminately, "*Kizlar!*" (girls) in a voice like stone being crushed to powder. If Songul is there, the other Turkish women teachers keep their heads down and continue reading or talking, and then Songul stands up and follows Serdar outside.

She cries sometimes as the flat-headed artist's nib slips and she has to begin all over again. So far she has completed two, which have been framed and hung in the corridor. I AM NOT ASKING YOU TO FIGHT, I AM ASKING YOU TO DIE hangs outside my classroom door. SOVEREIGNTY IS NOT GIVEN, IT IS TAKEN hangs outside

Séamus's door. As he passes by after class, Séamus pretends to lift it from the hook and throw it on the floor. He is anti-Ataturk at the moment, which means today. His opinions change as often as his books. Every day there's a different paperback winking from his jacket pocket as he walks down the corridor.

"Action Man," Tom calls him. He stops to watch Séamus go by: "Jesus, you'd think he was learning to walk."

I hadn't noticed until he mentioned it, but it's true. Séamus has a peculiar walk, throwing his legs out stiff before him. Even on duty days when he's supervising the playground, he's reading, eyes wide open as if to gobble up as much as possible. He has joined the British Council library and if you pass within ten yards of him he's likely to call abruptly – "Hey, what do you think of Denis Devlin? Did you know he lived in Istanbul?"

All this makes Songul clutch her hands and look over her shoulder at Serdar Bey's window. "Sea-mouse, please, we must to look after the children ... "

Then Séamus shoves his book furiously back into his pocket and walks up and down like a piece of overwound clockwork, almost bouncing off the wall at either end of the yard.

Irene calls him "uncouth". I think it's more innocence with a heavy varnish of bravado. After school on Friday when the flag is raised for the weekend and we have the National Anthem, Séamus stands with his hands in his pockets. The headmaster, standing before the bust of Ataturk, looks down at him with angry contempt.

The Ataturk cult is very strong in our school. In fact, looking at the children standing to attention in columns before the bronze bust (its plinth strewn with bay wreaths) I can imagine for the first time what the Roman cult of the emperor must have been like. I'm sure the Romans got it from the East, where authority is divine. In the same way, surely, that helps explain the East-West church schism. Arianism is logical if you regard God as unapproachably divine. The Greek and Armenian churches' custom of curtaining off the priest during the consecration, shielding the chalice with a silver cloth at the elevation, would come from the same idea.

My own Western mind was shocked during a visit by the mayor of Istanbul to our school recently. He's a powerful, watery-eyed, shrewd countryman, and after the official tour he wandered about the yard looking at things for himself. The headmaster was talking with someone at the other end of the yard and didn't notice at first the mayor turn to ask a question; as he turned a second time, the headmaster, a heavily built sixty-year-old, went pale with shame and broke into a sprint, arriving breathless ten seconds later to answer the enquiry.

1 December 1987

Winter suddenly in Istanbul, **exaggerating** the city's contrasts. Snow on the mosque domes, even on the minaret cones, so the skyline seems to melt into the sky. On earth the broken streets are shallow rivers of black slush mushed with orange gypsy horsedung.

"The *kip's* the place to be in this weather," Edmund says. "They've got these bloody big *solid fuel* stoves going. And there's the body heat. Yes, Deniz was warm *as* toast."

I never know what to say then. Sometimes I smile and say something disapproving. Other times I frown and ask how he got on. Although it doesn't matter much what I say, Edmund's reply is always the same: "Of course it's wrong, but what are you supposed to do? *Claw* the walls?"

Contemplating his pay day half kilo of banknotes: "I wonder how many whores you can get through for half a million liras?"

3 December 1987

Walking down a back street below Suleymaniye Mosque
this evening in the dark, I saw what I thought was a
powerful squat dog coming towards me. Just as I picked up
a stone, I realised it was a man: on all fours, hooves of rags
tied to his hands and knees, legs deformed and wasted
lying useless on his spine, spotless tiny bare feet jutting like
wings from his shoulder blades. I hid the stone behind my
back as he crawled past and disappeared underneath a
broken yard door.

5-10 December 1987

Dark grey days blurring into one another; the sky like wet
felt, slung so low you could poke it with a stick.

Geoffrey illustrates everything by examples from his own
schooldays. We went into town today in a *dolmush,* and as
Geoffrey fumbled for small change the driver smiled some
remark at another passenger.

Geoffrey, afterwards: "Yes, we had a chap like that at
my private school. Tried it on one day with a new master –
an Australian, but no fool. 'You don't seem to have too
much to keep your ears apart,' he said. 'Step outside the
door for a minute.' Gave him six of the best, not the sort
you come back shrugging after. Real crackers. Never had a
bit of trouble with Fiennes after that. That's right ... *Fiennes.*
Funny, almost forgot his name there for a minute ... "

Breedge and Dragan – she's Irish, he's Yugoslavian – had
an almighty row this evening upstairs. Doors slamming,
shouting, glasses smashing. It ended with his walking out.
He returned much later, quiet, with a bunch of flowers –

which didn't work: they sailed down past my window, landing right in front of Tom as he weaved his way back from Bostanci. As if it was the most natural thing in the world, he picked up the bouquet and brought it up to Stephanie.

At the bus stop today, talking with the poker-straight, white hair-line moustached old man who lives in the army tower block. Retired colonel; served all over Turkey; has lived in Switzerland; has a son in America, a daughter in Sweden. He nodded at a poor, tattooed countrywoman, pregnant, shoving half a dozen children onto the bus: "The educated, they have other things to do, but the poor – they have only the one action." Showing his special pass to the driver, he took his seat and took out a book to read – Poe's *Tales of Mystery and Imagination*.

Irene's smile: like a mouse sticking its head out of a hole.

"One night she went into the house of a distinguished citizen during the drinking, and it is said, before the eyes of all the guests she stood up on the couch near their feet, pulled up her dress in the most disgusting manner as she stood there, and brazenly displayed her lasciviousness. And though she brought three openings into service, she often found fault with Nature, grumbling because nature had not made the openings in her nipples wider than usual, so that she could devise another variety of intercourse in that region. Naturally, she was frequently pregnant, but by using pretty well all the tricks of the trade she was able to induce immediate abortion. Often in the theatre too, in full view of the people, she would throw off her clothes and stand naked in their midst, having only a girdle about her private parts and her groin – not, however, because she was ashamed to expose these also to the public, but because no

36

one is allowed to appear there absolutely naked: a girdle round the groin is compulsory. With this minimum covering she would spread herself and lie face upwards on the floor. Servants on whom this task had been imposed would sprinkle barley grains over her private parts, and geese trained for the purpose used to pick them off one by one with their bills and swallow them. Theodora, so far from blushing when she stood up again, actually seemed to be proud of this performance. For she was not only shameless herself, but did more than anyone else to encourage shamelessness ... "

(Procopius: *The Secret History* – of Constantinople under the Empress Theodora. Edmund picked up an old copy in the bazaar.)

Of the Emperor, Procopius writes:

"One of these days Justinian, if he is a man, will depart this life: if he is Lord of the Demons, he will lay his life aside.

Then all who chance to be still living will know the truth."

Beyazit, evening. Through a lace curtain of falling sleet – the furnace glow, sweat-skin gleam of the coppersmith's. *Hiss* as he stepped outside, put another pot on his stall.

11 December 1987

Séamus has flipped his lid. As usual in these cases, everyone says they saw it coming. I didn't. Everyone has stories now about his ways of keeping discipline in class – making children kneel with arms outspread etc. Though I must say I had my doubts. One day I passed his door between classes and saw the entire blackboard filled by a definition of the word "radio": "A mechanism for the reception of signals transmitted on sound waves from a central device ... " Even the handwriting seemed a bit hysterical.

"More like Arabic," Tom said, who doesn't even try to hide his delight now. He wasn't so amused when he found that he has to take some of Séamus's classes. Séamus has been suspended. It seems he almost throttled a boy in class, or beat him up – it isn't clear which, but the word has flown about the school. The playground this morning was full of children acting it out: pushing each other up against the railings, miming punches, stranglings, flailing fists and then clapping their hands to their heads and running away in clockwork strides. It's not clear if Séamus ran out of the class or not. The senior, *Lise* children with a better grasp of English say that afterwards Séamus walked back to the rostrum, sat down, put his feet up on the table and read a book of poetry. They even know the name of the writer – "Paul Durjan." (C is pronounced J in Turkish).

Dr Norbert is in his element, acting the diplomatic monsignor. He stayed in our wardrobe this evening and when I was passing his drawer and heard him discussing it with Grant, I dropped in to hear the latest.

"He's gone."

"What a shime," Grant frowned.

"Gone?" I said.

"Well, he's still here, but he's got the sack. They wanted him on the next plane out but I managed to – " Norbert held out his glass to Grant, gestured to the table. "I'll have some more of that wine, ducks." He likes to spin out a story. "Oooh, that's better." (Camp.) "Yes ... " (Fruity) "I managed to get a 'stay of execution'. All those mothers in their head-dresses were up at the Pasha's office saying he shoo be poo in preeson. I explained that wasn't how *we* dealt with these things. 'Umut Bey,' I said. 'My title is Co-ordinator of English Teachers. That is my job. I co-ordinate.

If you can find someone to do the job better, if you can find someone with contacts in every English-speaking country in the world, if you can find someone willing to fly to London, New York, Dublin, Melbourne, Edinburgh, Toronto and interview new teachers, then tell me. I won't mind. I won't stand in your way. I ... '"

"Ooh my!" Grant primped a hand on his hip and minced away.

"Get her!" (Queen.) "So – " (Oxford) " – we did some horse-trading. Séamus gets the boot, but he also gets a month's pay in lieu of notice and he can stay here for a week until he decides what to do. Not bad at all," (Irish) "at all."

"*Bashka muh?*" Grant held up the bottle, tipped another glass for himself.

"No," Dr Norbert said shortly, in his own voice. He's a careful drinker.

13 December 1987

Grant, a polished young Australian about Séamus's age, was Séamus's best friend. In the minibus in the morning they sat beside each other, Grant talking, Séamus listening. That way, we've all learned about Grant. He's descended from a famous Fenian exile who later got on very well for himself in Australia. His family owns a sheep property twenty miles long, thirty miles wide. Grant ran away from boarding-school to become a musician ("I ribilled") and played piano in a bar. Not for too long, though; after six months of that he entered the music conservatory, took a diploma and began composing. Commissions fell into his lap. Newspaper and television interviews followed. Already, his work has been performed in Sydney Opera House. He has a girlfriend in Australia, a simple girl but the most open, tender human being he ever knew. And then suddenly one day Grant woke up and said to himself: "Look, I have everything – money, success, fame, love. Why don't I just walk away from it all, leave it, see if it's real?"

And Séamus used to shrill, "Right!"

Now Séamus is shrilling up and down the corridors alone. When Grant comes back from school these evenings, he just disappears. Again tonight I can hear Séamus upstairs knocking at his door, calling, "Yo! Grant, it's me. GRANT! It's me – Séamus!" But there's no reply.

I have to admire him for one thing – he never comes knocking on my door. He walked past me on the corridor this evening, silent, white-faced. I'm Irish: to be avoided.

14 December 1987

Blizzard. Murat Bey, the gym teacher, took a lift in our minibus, and to show thanks passed around a bag of pistachio nuts. Specimen of conversation –

Songul: "We say *Fistik*."

Irene: "We say *Nut*."

Songul, blushing: "We say if girl is beautiful she is *Fistik*."

Deirdre: "You say if a girl is beautiful she is a *Nut?*"

Tom: "We say a *Cracker*."

Geoffrey dropped up about ten o'clock. Two hours tonight, spent mostly talking about his family. Through his wife he's related to Virginia Woolf – "My step-father-in-law, if you can work that one out, was Edgar, Leonard's brother. 'What a crew,' he used to say, '*what a crew*.'"

They've no children.

15 December 1987

Séamus left this morning. We were setting off for school when he appeared at the door, rucksack on back, an orange Penguin jutting from his anorak pocket. He looked up at the sky, pulled his hood over his head and walked off down the slushy street.

17 December 1987

Istanbul sights.

People sleeping: head in arms, at tables, desks, counters; in parked cars, on trains, buses, ferry boats.

Circumcised boys in celebration dress: white suit, blood red silk cape, silver-paper crown and sceptre.

Stone, marble ancient columns: embedded whole, ends showing like great bullets, in rubble walls; holding up clothes lines, fences; broken into drums and used as curbstones; capitals white-washed, serving as seats in mosque yards.

Hawkers: on the streets, in the ferries, the trains, selling biros, lemon-squeezers, anything; the old countryman by the railway station selling hopelessly cured fox pelts.

Foreign faces: German, English, American; at once weaker and stronger-looking; they stand out as pale blobs, but deep stamped with the lines of "individuality".

19 December 1987

Whenever she has a free period, Irene vanishes lest she be asked to stand in for someone else. Now Séamus has gone, she doesn't even return to the staff room between classes. Today, Friday, is a full day for everyone, so she had to be found. The headmaster went to search, no easy job. Classes were over, we were all going back to the staffroom when he returned, coming up the basement stairs followed by Irene, her face blue with cold.

Conversation in the minibus going home turned on the

difference between English and Irish diction.

Songul – "I think the English speak more loudly … "

Irene – "But they weren't oppressed."

20 December 1987

Letter from R.: " … Thanks for your card. Whatever else you've escaped, it isn't the church. Substitute spires for minarets and it could be the Dublin skyline … "

21 December 1987

In a bar in Istiklal Caddesi.

Life being what it is, men dream of another life; life being what it is, women try to make the most of this life. Both are right, but ne'er the twain shall meet.

23 December 1987

Salih works at the vegetable stall outside the supermarket across the road – 7.30am to 8.30pm. A tall handsome Kurd, about forty. Looks sixty. Face as grey as his moustache by evening time. Each time he sits down, his head drops and he falls asleep. When he wakes up thirty seconds later, he shakes his head and murmurs "*Kötü*" (bad) and lights another cigarette. Then he stands up, winces, and takes my vegetables and weighs them. Then the grace notes; spinning a cone from newspaper with one twirl as he pours the vegetables in with the other hand; twirling the top of the cone shut with a flick of finger and thumb. Then we have our pidgin Turkish-English conversation, usually about how Salih can get an English or German work visa; but about Christmas this evening, Salih shaking his head quizzically from side to side as I tried to explain.

"*Büyük tatil,*" (big holiday).

"Christ-mas?" He shook his head again.

"Christ?" I tried again. "Jesus?"

"*Yok.*" He tilted back his head, clicked his tongue with Mediterranean never-heard-of-him finality. "*Iyi aksamlar.*" (Good evening.) Bowing his head to one side, fluttering a hand on his heart, he sat down again and his head dropped between his knees.

7-14 January 1988

Instead of Christmas holidays we have a winter break. Edmund went to Chios, eager as a schoolboy. Grant and some others went to Bursa for the skiing. The rest went further south after the sun. Irene must have packed everything she has: I passed her this evening on the snowy front steps, dragging a colossal suitcase out to a taxi.

"Wintry weather," I said. "Where are you off to?"

"Isn't it freezing?" She wears sunglasses against the snow. She climbed into the back seat and sped away.

I'm not going anywhere since I'm sending most of my money home. Each pay day my Turkish liras buy less and less Sterling. In fact, you can't get Sterling now. This month the bank manager hid when I appeared, sent out his secretary, who lied to me in excellent English and sold me Deutsche Marks, and I posted them off. I have just enough to keep me for the month – a good incentive to sit in and write.

Began well. Ten o'clock I was at the typewriter, in my diving-bell, going down down down to the ocean floor of childhood; looking through the thick glass window, identifying monster shapes, brilliant flecks of life; realising how arbitrary, invented, any view of the past is. Yet how that past can still bite. I felt myself flush as I described a morning thirty years ago, when as I trotted across the school in huge new short trousers, Father Grenan bestowed

43

his smouldering smile on me and murmured, "Still growing, Adrian?" I had smiled back and gone on trotting, the smart spreading slowly like a nettle sting. (Half an hour trying to fit this in, but it stuck out like a sore thumb and I had to cut it: art has no place for revenge.)

It was dark when I surfaced, ravenously hungry. After dinner I took my drink and cigarettes down to the TV room and tuned into an English film with Turkish subtitles, a nice easy way to learn the language.

Around nine o'clock Tom strolled in, a bottle of raki in hand. We both said the same thing together – "I thought you were gone!" – laughing. Tom poured himself a screamer of a glass of neat raki, tipping in just enough water to make it milky, and lay back in an armchair, the yellow boots on the table, to watch the film. "The McGuffin Factor?" he said after about thirty seconds. "Good old Charles Dance." He seems to have seen every film ever made. Like most things, it began well, then stumbled. We began to chat.

"Where's Stephanie?" I said.

"Went home to see her parents for the week. Sussex-by-the-Sea and all that."

"Still together?"

"All in order. She asked me what I wanted. I told her to bring me back a pound of rashers."

"What did you do all day? I never heard you about."

"Slept." He rubbed his thighs lewdly. "Needed a bit of a rest."

"Lucky you."

Pause. "Tell us – do you enjoy making love?"

"Very much, I'm afraid."

"Yeah ... yeah." He turned to watch the film. We watched it to the end. Tom's bottle was empty. We finished mine and he said, "Do you feel up to Bostanci?"

I could hardly stand, but it was the first day of the holidays, I had done a good day's work. It was snowing gently as we walked down to the taxi rank.

"Thank God for these boots," Tom said, adding as usual, "don't go with the blazer, I know."

"Where did you get them?" They crunched through the new snow.

"Dublin. Norbert was telling me what winter was like here. I should have known after Italy."

We got into a cab, talking about previous jobs as we slithered and skidded down to the sea shore. I'm a tame stork compared with Tom: he seems to have taught English in every country from Holland down to Italy. It was icy cold, the stars as small and sharp-looking as needle points. The lights on the Princes' Island where Norbert lives seemed just as distant.

"Hi-lo, Tom!"

"How's it going, Ahmed!" Tom put an arm around my shoulder – he looks and acts the older one. "You met Adrian. He's from Ireland too."

"*Ireland.*" Ahmed pressed fingers about his thumb, denoting perfection. "Johnny Logan. OK!"

A man wearing an expensive grey coat like a cloak on his shoulders moved to the door and Ahmed turned from us quickly to give him the full blast of Turkish deference, bowing and calling farewells. A retinue of shabbier men followed and Ahmed flapped a hand, beckoning one of them over, quizzed him in Turkish, got back two English words in reply.

"Hole-ding company," he repeated to us, then turned to watch the grey-cloaked figure get into a black BMW.

"Really?" Tom's voice slid into posh nasal.

"Really." Ahmed nodded. "Hole-ding company ... " He repeated the words like a mantra to himself as he drew our glasses of beer. "*Yok.*" He thuh-thuhhed and chucked back his chin in refusal as I put my hand in my pocket.

"Decent old skin, Ahmed." Tom slipped back into his natural voice.

"Really?" I imitated the drawl.

"Ah fuck off!" He raised his glass.

"Good luck."

That was how the week went. I spent the day writing and Tom slept. In the evenings we watched TV and then went down to Bostanci. One day Inci, one of the Turkish women teachers at our school, telephoned, the call shrilling through the empty building. By the time I got downstairs, Tom had answered it; standing in his pyjamas, smoothing down his hair as he repeated her instructions. "Right. Outside St Sophia. Great. One o'clock. See you there."

She had invited him to stay with her family for the rest of the week, he told me that evening. "Probably thinks I'm lonely."

"Or she likes you?"

"Never thought of that. Anyhow, it sounds bloody OK. They've a place by the sea somewhere over in Thrace."

"What happened?" I said when he appeared in the TV room the following evening.

"What?"

"Inci? Did she not show up?"

"Shit." He snapped his fingers. "I clean forgot."

He had slept it out. I suppose that was why he was so full of energy in the bar at night. Sometimes it was two in the morning when we got home. By the end of the week I had given up working.

"How do you do it?" I said one night. "Sleep all day?"

"You get used to it when you're in the catering game. I spent ten years at that." I remembered then where I had seen Tom's sort of pallor before – in short stints I'd done as a student in hotel kitchens. Tom was at it from the time he

46

left home until he drifted into English language teaching. We leaned on the high table by the stove, looking out the window at the snow as we chatted. Every night a gypsy girl was outside selling flowers, keeping her fingers from freezing by preparing more for sale, paring off the stem leaves, binding the stalks with white cotton thread. As she held out a bunch before each passerby, I could hear through the glass her hoarse cry, "*Çiçek! Çiçek!*" above Tom's voice.

Apparently he left home when he had done his Leaving, a disappointment to his father, who was a university librarian. Set off to London, learnt a few things while he was washing dishes and went on to another hotel. "Told them I was a prep chef and they paid me at that. I picked up a bit more and left. Next hotel I called myself a salad chef. Got onto the grill next and so on and so fucking forth. Ahmed! *Iki bira, lutfen!*" He gazed out the window. "You wouldn't believe the things you see in the catering game. Do you know London?"

"I lived around Notting Hill once."

"Good old Notting Hill. I had a gaff there once. That flick we saw the other night – 'The McGuffin Factor' – they shot some of that right outside my door. *Choc merci*, Ahmed! Just this room at the back of the house. Looked out on the back of another house. There was this girl – Christ, after a while I was looking out for her every night. Got to the stage I'd take the fucking taxi home. She used to come in from work about the same time as myself, turn on all the lights, take off all her clothes and lie on a couch watching TV. Lonely, I suppose. One night I came home and she was gone. A fucking Paki family there instead. I left after that. Fucking freezing kip it was too."

"But why did you leave home?"

"The old man. The old man was a ballocks. Here, it's too cold for beer. Let's get the old raki."

So we bought a half bottle and Tom went on about his father – no worse than lots of others, I thought: he drank and when he was drunk he was nasty; but Tom wasn't letting him off that lightly. After a few more glasses he was imitating him. Ahmed stopped polishing glasses and leaned over the counter, beaming, as Tom clipped his thumbs behind his blazer lapels and swayed before an imaginary blazing fire, his voice screwed up into an outrageously fruity country accent:

"'I had Professor McGrath in to see me today. There's a gentleman for you. 'Mr Flynn,' he said, 'Mr Flynn, I'm giving a course on China this term. Now what books do we have on China?' Oho, I was as quick as him. 'Professor McGrath,' I said, 'Professor McGrath, do you mean *Taiwan*? Or do you mean *The People's Republic of China*?'" Tom leaned on the table again, looking out the window, muttering "The cunt."

"I remember old McGrath," I said. "He came up to UCD once to give a lecture."

"Did he? You didn't see the obituary he wrote when the old man died? I suppose you read *The Irish* fucking *Times*?"

"Now and then."

Tom stepped back again, thumbs in imaginary waistcoat pockets this time, his voice turning into such a good imitation of what I remembered of Professor McGrath that I wondered if his version of his father wasn't as accurate. Ahmed not quite so happy-looking now as Tom's voice rose and customers turned from the TV to stare.

"Whether it was a blank day on the bog with the gun, or a fruitless evening-rise on the river, there was ample compensation always in Bill Flynn's company. Witty, expansive, malicious sometimes – but quickly redeemed by the kind remark. 'Sure there's no harm in him,' he would add. Or '*De mortuis nil nisi bonum*.' For Bill, the old tag's stricture is superfluous. To his wife Mona, to his children, to his many university colleagues, we extend heartfelt sympathy in their loss. *Ar dheis Dé go raibh a hanam* ... ' I wouldn't mind meeting the same McGrath some day. I'd stuff that up his arse for him."

I had such a hangover next morning that I didn't even try to work. Besides, a chainsaw was roaring in the waste ground outside my window. Someone is going to squeeze an apartment block in there and some family has bought up the timber, a dozen old pear trees. I went down to watch. In half an hour Papa had everything felled and sliced, laid out on the snow like cucumber on a dish. Then Mama and the children got to work loading it into a trailer: everything – twigs, splinters, mistletoe tangles, even the sawdust, until there was just the scent of the chainsaw fumes floating over the trampled snow. When I went back up the stairs, I noticed that my door was wide open; I had left it an inch ajar.

Someone was walking about inside. The footsteps went into my bedroom, returned. I risked a look around the door and saw Tom sitting down in my chair. I opened my mouth to speak, but no words came. He examined my typewriter, looked at a blank sheet of paper I had put in – a token of determination – then he sat back in the chair and looked up at the ceiling. I tiptoed back down the corridor, returning noisily, coughing.

"There y'are." He was standing again, blushing awkwardly. His voice ran into the nasal drawl. "I was thinking of going into the flicks. *Angel Heart*'s on at The Moda, if you're interested."

Afterwards, we wandered around Kadiköy looking for some bar Tom wanted to show me. The Turks build their year around summer in much the same way the Irish build their year around winter. Winter in Turkey is an aberration to be ignored. The melted snow ran down the hilly streets, found nowhere to go and lay in floods at the corner. It's fifteen years since I was last in Istanbul, but I would swear the same planks were laid on the same uprooted cobblestones over the same floods. Each car sends a brown wave crashing against the shop windows. "As the shepherd said to the sheepdog – " Tom has a nice line in kitchen sink sayings, " – let's get the flock out of here." We ducked into a second-hand bookshop, pretending to be interested in the shelves by a glowing-pink tin stove. Second-hand bookshops in Istanbul – maybe everywhere, if you could stand back and see with an outsider's eye – are like archaeological sites. On the bottom shelf – a stratum of old Ottoman Arabic; then the French presence – heaps of yellow paperbacks, and the Italian; then a layer of German textbooks; then the English. On top and most expensive – American paperbacks.

Three's No Crowd: The Story of Troilism was selling at 10,000 liras. How far books travel! Washed up in remote shores like old shoes and bottles. A Welsh Bible. A copy of *Jude the Obscure*, annotated in beautifully pencilled Armenian. *Ulysses* was there, in Turkish, and warming my feet at the stove I read a page.

"Mirhaba, Bloom. Nerede giddeorsunuz?"

"Mirhaba, McCoy. Hiç bir yere … "

"What do you make of that?" Tom said.

"It's great in Turkish."

"I read it once, in Amsterdam. Do you know what got me? Your man Bloom. A bit of a wet smack, isn't he?"

"Why?"

"Well, tell me one place he even raises his fucking voice?"

"He's meant to be a good man."

"I suppose so. Jesus, but there's no such thing as a man who doesn't lose his temper."

The shopkeeper approached hopefully and I put the book back on the shelf. An old man, educated in the days

50

when French was the international language, he spoke testily as we made for the door.

"Pourquoi vous perdez mon temps? Pourquoi?"

Tom: "I may be poor but I'm not queer."

Everyone arrived back from holidays at the last possible minute. Next morning on the way to school everyone slept in the minibus. It wasn't until we were coming home that they woke up, telling stories of hair-raising ten- and fourteen-hour bus journeys up from the south. Irene surprised everyone, telling us she'd been to Egypt.

"You're a dark horse." Even Tom raised his eyebrows. "What part?" – always a dangerous question to ask Irene.

"The Cairo area." Her mouth shut like a button. Although she opened up again when we got stuck in the Bosphorous traffic jam, telling us that she had seen Dr Norbert riding on a camel about the Pyramids. "And do you know who he was with? You know that Scottish boy who teaches in Semia Shakir ... ?" She tittered into her mitten. "Isn't he a scream!"

By the time we got home everyone was silent again, holding onto memories of the warm south or the Bursa ski slopes. In the same way, I found it hard to let go my week's drinking. I went down to the television room tonight as usual, taking my bottle with me. I met Tom on the way. He walked past me without a word, without even a glance at me, up the marble stairs to Stephanie's room.

CHAPTER FOUR

20 January 1988

EVERY EVENING THE SAME SOUNDS: BATHWATER RUNNING OUT, THE babble of radios; the same smells – olive oil … garlic frying; the hum of the lift then and the clack of flipflops along the corridor as visiting begins. Our tower block is wedged into the garden of an old Turkish timber farmhouse whose black shingled roof is right below my window, its chimney puffing a yellow curtain of lignite smoke. Every night after the last call to prayer, the same flurry of sounds down there: squawks from a few old hens and a cock as they are locked up, the rattle of tin basins stood out to dry, the grey-bearded skull-capped old man talking to himself as he walks about his patch of clay; clatters upstairs as his wife draws the shutters in for the night – her eyes mechanically avoiding mine. Darkness then and a million lights like the moon's reflection on the sea; each tower block topped by a red warning stab. Then I straighten my back and get up from my typewriter like a devotee from his idol; take my bottle and glass and cigarettes and go next door to visit Edmund. We visit each other most nights.

"Ah!" A look of total surprise. "Come *in*." He opens the door fully as if showing me into a baronial hall. "Sit *down*." Takes the newspaper, loaf of bread or whatever off a chair. He sits on the other hard chair by the table. The rest of the room is left unexplored, as clean and empty as the day he moved in. On the floor, about the table legs, are brimming bags of rubbish waiting to be thrown out. The smell is getting noticeable. A single, overhead glaring light bulb.

Everyone devotes his life to something. Consciously or unconsciously, for reasons known or unknown, we end up with a chief concern. Writing in my case, I believe. In Edmund's, surely – ideal beauty.

"Edmund Rossetti Morgan" says his passport cover, smeared with dried egg yolk, lying in the foothills of a heap of books, bottles, biscuits, soupbowls of cigarette butts. He got his middle name from his father, a lover of the Pre-Raphaelites. We talk about them sometimes; we talk about everything, as we sit drinking, each from his own bottle. Edmund is drinking a cheap liqueur at the moment, *Altin*, the Turkish for 'gold': neat alcohol with flecks of real gold (14 carat it says on the label) floating through it. When he shakes the bottle, it looks like a child's snowstorm globe.

Everything about Edmund speaks of the individual will: fine flared nostrils, a deep scored line controlling each corner of his mouth, very long pale fingers (shining the way unwashed skin shines, bluish) that turn up slightly at the tips. No wonder, I think sometimes when I look at him, that England could produce those novels, the sort I have begun so often and abandoned, where pencil-sharp characters do, or do not do, as they will. Although when I mentioned that to him one night, he argued that the very opposite was true, that English novels are about anything but individual will.

"They're social novels. *English* novels are about society."

"The individual in society."

"Yes, but he's a very different individual from a *character* in Homer or Virgil." Edmund can never talk for very long without referring to the Classics.

"But hadn't he a social side too?"

"Yes, but his individuality was social. Or, if you like, his socialness was individual."

"And now?"

"It's different now. *Mmm.*" Edmund – he bites his nails incessantly – manoeuvred a new-grown splinter between his teeth, nipping it off and nibbling it to dust. "It's the difference between a pot of stew on the stove; and when it's cold – you know, when there's just a *lid* of hard grease on top, and water underneath … " I wasn't surprised when he abandoned this image. Edmund's cooking is basic. On the floor about the table the remains of his dinner lie scattered: six boiled eggshells.

His father, he tells me, was working-*class*, a Liverpool Non-conformist. A printer by trade, he set up on his own when he married. He used to go to art classes at night, drawing from the antique. "It's the Laocoon tonight, Edmund!" – as he sharpened his pencils, took down his sketchbook and hurried off to the Institute. When he died, Edmund inherited hundreds of drawings of gods, goddesses, heroes and heroines. "They're probably still there." He sold the house, left all in it to the buyer. "I cannot bear the responsibility *of* possessions," he says. Night after night his father went drawing, and then it began eating into the days as he took up engraving; the business going downhill as he made plates of the old masters. He told Edmund he had discovered a new technique, but it seems he never got it quite right. In the end the business collapsed and he had to scrape a living engraving, of all things, coffin plates. (Yet he had one success – isn't that really all any man has? A drawing he made of some ancient stone cross was bought by the Walker Gallery.)

In the meantine, Edmund had turned to Catholicism, taken instruction and been received into "the *Roman* church". His mother, Scotch Presbyterian, was shocked, but made the best of it and sent Edmund to the Jesuit school in Liverpool. By the time he left there, Edmund was set on being a priest.

"But then the War came *along*. I joined the RAF ... "

"Like Geoffrey."

"I was a *mechanic*."

That explains his love of machines. Talking about a compass, a radio aerial, a Lancaster bomber's engine, his face brightens, as it does when he talks of Byzantine ikons.

"And then girls came on the scene, *and* ... "

"You lost your vocation?"

"No – " dropping a butt into a glass, tipping in a drop of *Altin* and thoughtfully watching it sizzle, " – I just stopped believing *in* God."

And yet listening to him talk of girls, he sounds like a priest, grave and devoted. Talking about his sister one night, he mentioned that she had married and gone to live in colonial Africa, summed her up as a "good-time girl".

"But so are you, Edmund!" I laughed.

Edmund shook his head soberly. "But she wasn't serious about it."

After the War he got a serviceman's scholarship to Dublin, to Trinity College where, somehow, his vocation was replaced by a love of classical literature. Higher up the slopes of rubbish on his table lie filthy thumbed copies of Ovid and Horace. Then it was back to England, to a job in a grammar school. He met a women, they settled down together, taking off every summer to travel Europe.

"I *need* the classical tradition." That's Edmund's preface or tailpiece to each account of classical sites visited. For Edmund, the classical tradition continued up to the nineteenth century – to the Pre-Raphaelites, in fact – so he has done a great deal of travelling. He walked once from Rome to Palestrina, twenty-five miles up in the Sabine Hills, to see his favourite composer's birthplace. We digress sometimes to talk about the Palestrina choir in Dublin.

"Heavenly music," I agree.

"Heavenly music." Edmund lights another cigarette. "To make love *to*."

I get nervous sometimes as he smiles his thin red-lipped smile and takes off his filthy glasses and rubs his pink eyelids.

Then he left his English woman. "It was her *smell*. I just never liked the smell of her body. But you can't tell someone that, can you? Metallic? Acid? Something like that ... "

She never forgave him.

Then the grammar schools began to drop Latin. They gave him a job teaching Civics instead. "But *I* wasn't interested." He left, answered an advertisement and, as suddenly, he had a job teaching English in Morocco. The few books are French school editions he picked up there. These and his holdall, still half unpacked on the floor amongst the rubbish bags, are all he seems to have. There's an old Latin missal too that he thumbs through absently as he talks. By now I know all about his favourite girl, Houriah, a Moroccan whore. There was a Fatima as well ... Zeyna ... Selma ...

"*Persicos odi, puer, apparatus* ... " He looks around at the chaos. "I picked up this bird in Casa one weekend. I used to go over there for a change sometimes ... " He takes another drink, picks a speck of gold dust from the glass and holds it on his fingertip, gazing at it. "It turned out she'd been to the French convent school. She knew her Horace ... *Displicent nexae philyra coronae*. Quoted the whole thing to me in bed. Fatouche. That was her name. Nice girl, Fatouche." He drops the butt into a glass, tips in more *Altin* and watches it turn into a tiny blue flame. "Good *stuff*, this *Altin*. Get a nice buzz from it … Fatouche – I used to see quite a bit of her afterwards. One night then I woke up and she was screaming. Tearing at my skin with her nails. I got a bloody fright! I couldn't control her." He has drawn up his shirt to show me a long pink-ridged scar down his side. "She said afterwards she didn't know what had come over her. Beautiful creature. Beautiful … "

Edmund himself drew blood one day, clouted a boy in class, knocked a scab off his ear which bled all over the desk. I offered the only advice I had: to stay up on the rostrum at all costs.

"It's all right. I wouldn't lose my temper with one of those little buggers. I'm afraid I have a very *bad* temper."

"Oh I doubt it, Edmund."

"Yes. I've hardly ever lost it, but if I did – I could *kill*." He smiles and flicks through the missal again, shaking his head. "I don't know. *I* don't know … "

"Time for bed," I say then, my ears ringing from raki.

I'd hate to see his real temper. In the mornings I hear him moving about his kitchen, dropping a saucepan sometimes, or perhaps tripping over a rubbish bag, and then there's a shout, a scream almost, I can hear clean through the wall – "OH SHIT!"

CHAPTER FIVE

25 January 1988

SATURDAY. THERE WAS A KNOCK ON MY DOOR THIS MORNING: I was surprised to see Irene outside. I said, "Come in," but she stood back quickly and said, "No no." She looked over my shoulder into the room, saying, "And you get the sun. I have to go out on the balcony even to see it. I'll tell you – " another step backwards, " – I just came down to ask ... do you know anything about Mass times in Kadiköy?"

I had been there. "Ten thirty on Sunday," I said.

"Ten thirty. And – " she smiled, " – where exactly is the church?"

"Turn left at the market and go up the hill. You'll see a street on the left at the top – Cem Sokak. It's down there behind a high yellow wall."

"Left at the market. Cem Sokak. Thanks a million." You never have to repeat anything to Irene. She folded her arms and then, to my surprise, offered a piece of information about herself. "My mother's coming out for a holiday next week and ... you know how it is!"

No one knew better, although I thought that by now –

Irene must be at least thirty – she would have settled that question.

"I'll have to run. I left the kettle on." She scooted upstairs, silent in her blue fluffy slippers.

27 January 1988

When we get back from school there is a rush always to the hall where our post is laid out. Grant was the lucky one this evening – a picture postcard. I was intrigued to see him read it and, as he went out the door again down to the supermarket, crumple it up and drop it in the street. It was still there when I went shopping later on and I picked it up. It was from Séamus.

1 February 1988

St Brigid's Day and there's light in the evenings now and spring in the light. Ali got stuck in an especially bad traffic jam as we drove home from school and I got out to walk. He must have taken it as a comment on his driving. Accelerating up onto the grass divide, crashing down into the other lane, weaving through oncoming traffic, hand on horn, cutting back onto the right side again beyond the traffic lights, he vanished in a cloud of exhaust up the Bosphorous highway.

Driving in Turkey is not a science, more a branch of the expressionist arts. (Until the other day when I saw a minibus brake and a passenger fly out of his seat head-first against the windscreen, I thought the blood-tinged wads of cotton wool taped to men's foreheads were to do with some local infection.) The tourist Turkish flags flying from standards along the old walls give the impression of an embattled city; the hucksters along the ramparts like remnants of a pathetic last stand against the invasion of cars, lorries, buses. Blaring horns, flashing lights, waving fists and shouting, they pour in the breach made by Vatan Caddesi.

It was safer to walk on the rampart, sweet with the smell of human excrement. The broken walls and towers are squatters' homes. An old man in a gateway struck a match to his pipe and a Greek inscription appeared in the lintel. Television aerials and hammered tin stovepipes stick out of mediaeval loopholes. Bugs Bunny music mixed with the bleat of sheep grazing down the slope. Lower down, the great filled-up moat is carved into kitchen gardens full of onions and lettuces, guarded by chained dogs. The better kept a city's ancient remains are, the less they have to do with the living reality of the city. If that rule of thumb is true, then Istanbul is still deep in communication with its past.

I was enjoying the luxury of thinking and strolling when another dog began to bark at me from the moat. No rattling chain this time; instead the bark got louder and then up out of the dusk he appeared, a mongrel mastiff, the bark turning into a snarling bay as he made for me. I had just time to take up a stone, a pineapple-sized piece of old city wall, and throw it at him. He was so close I could hardly have missed. For a moment I thought I had killed him; then, blood running off his head, he staggered onto his feet again and went howling back down the rampart slope. Not much steadier, I climbed up to the ridge and went through an ancient arch into the city.

These are the times civilisation seems beautiful. In there on the muddy inner vallum the hucksters' barrows are piled with socks, bras, french letters; cassette music blaring, kebabs roasting. The evening call to prayer unfolded and a few old men made off down an alley at a half run. In the half light the mosque stood perfect: dome rising naturally from the four walls, the circle squared, the great problem solved; carried upwards then by the minaret tapering to a point invisible, where the gold crescent appeared clear-cut against a dark frosty evening blue. In sudden gratitude, I bought two dresses off a barrow for my daughters at home.

I was going up the stairs to my flat when I met Irene coming down, flanked by women unmistakably Irish. She stopped to introduce her mother and aunt – large, obviously sisters, in new overcoats.

"We're off to see the whirling dervishes!" The aunt had a Cork accent. "Isn't that it, Irene?"

"They're on in the Hilton," Irene's mother said. Between them, Irene seemed a slight, pale figure.

"The Hilton! Oh I beg your pardon!" The aunt's laugh echoed down the marble stairs. She had new shoes too, of expensive flesh-coloured leather.

Irene looked at her watch. "We'd better go, Mammy."

"Aren't we on holidays! Amn't I rushing all my life!" Her mother turned to me and my parcel. "And you've been shopping too?"

I explained and she said, "Sure we'll bring that back for you, won't we, Sheila?"

Sheila didn't seem all that enthusiastic, saying something about a Turkish rug and baggage allowances. She took my parcel and weighed it in her hands.

"Sure we can always let on we didn't know!" Irene's mother laughed. Irene's mouth opened into a little smile and said, "Leave it in to me on Saturday. They're going the day after."

"Wouldn't it be lovely to stay!"

"Maybe we'd win the Lotto!"

"We'll be late … " Irene led the way downstairs.

3 February 1988

Every morning the crash down in the boiler room as Mustapha smashes coal-boulders with his sledgehammer.

Geoffrey, doing his *News for the Deaf* routine: "It. Is. Very. Noisy … "

Mustapha: "OK!"

5 February 1988

Hadn't been in Irene's flat before. Faces north, as she said. Stack of *Irish Independent*s inside door. Chairs arranged around the radiator. Tomorrow's breakfast things set out on the counter and the lunch she brings to school already packed in the Tupperware box. I handed over my parcel, then she invited me to stay for tea.

"None of that Turkish stuff!" her mother said. "Do you like Barry's?" She had an apron on and was setting out plates of sandwiches and sweet biscuits on the table.

"How were the whirling dervishes?" I asked.

"Ah, all right. I thought they'd be better." Aunt Sheila turned up the corner of a sandwich. "Where's that cucumber I bought? I'm dying to see if it's the same as at home."

"Sure you never eat cucumber at home."

"What are you saying?"

"I left it on the draining-board."

"I'll get it." Irene got up.

"Can't you sit down. It's all right. Don't bother!"

"It's no trouble!" Irene got up, laughing and shaking off her aunt's restraining hand.

"And this is the parcel?" Her mother turned to me. "Two little girls you have? How can you bear to leave them? Irene … "

The snap of the knife in the kitchen stopped. "What?"

"Is that window open? I feel a draught somewhere … "

"It's the bedroom – "

"Don't stir. I'll – "

"No, I'll shut it!"

62

"Wait till you're ready! It's all right!"

"I'm ready!" Irene hurried in with a plate of cucumber sandwiches, then hurried into her bedroom.

"How's she getting on?" Mother and aunt turned quickly to me.

"Great."

"She's a *gem*," Aunt Sheila said.

"Wasn't she great to do it," her mother said. "It'll be something to look back on ... Irene!"

"Coming!"

"Did you make any enquiries yet about your flight home?" Holding up a hand, bending one by one short pointed white fingers, her mother intoned, "February March April May June. Five months and you'll be home ... "

6 February 1988

Irene's mother and aunt left this morning. Irene's eyes were red, from crying, I suppose, as she got into the minibus. She sat alone adding up her *fiches* with her pocket calculator. A great idea, these *fiches*: every shop has to give you one, a receipt for every purchase, and at the end of the month you send them all – except those for drink and tobacco – to a government department, which gives you back about ten percent of the cash total. It's a curb on the black market and a consolation prize for paying the original VAT. The rest of the tax goes to the social welfare system. But since only those with social welfare numbers can claim *fiche* money, there's a brisk black market: people who cannot claim give their receipts to those who can, in return for a cut of the pay-out. At the end of the month everyone is getting their *fiches* in order and adding them up. In the traffic jams you see men take the big brown envelope from the dashboard and do their tots.

Irene does hers day by day, this morning dealing with

all the receipts her mother and aunt left behind. Mouth so tight her lips are invisible, eyes flicking up and down the column of figures, her fingers as fast on the calculator, she had finished before we reached the Bosphorous traffic jam. Looking at her, I realised suddenly that Irene will not be going home in June. I felt certain somehow. There is a natural justice in the world. Irene will defeat her mother and aunt because they have armed her. Just as their *fiches* will bring Irene money, their weapons – deviousness, underground manipulation, whatever – will become her weapons, as sure as minus by minus makes plus.

12 February 1988

Salih standing on the supermarket steps taking a one-minute break, thumb-flicking a coin in the air and catching it in his work-mashed hand. As I passed, I noticed that it was an ancient one. "Byzance," – he showed it to me. We had our pidgin Turkish-English conversation and he told me he had found it as a boy digging on his father's farm. They own one hectare down near the Syrian border. "The only money I ever got from the land!" He laughed, amazed to hear himself say a full English sentence. The coin showed Christ's head and the Greek words "King of Kings". The boss appeared and he slipped it back into his pocket and began dashing water on the vegetables to make them sparkle.

(Water everywhere in Istanbul – about, through the city: Marmara lapping the eastern walls, Bosphorous breaking on Seraglio Point, Golden Horn slap-slapping along the fishermen's quays; bucketfuls spilling from balconies, sluicing out doorways; taps dripping in mosque courtyards; welling up through broken roads; the building-workers hosing down their feet in the evening.)

One advantage, or disadvantage, of being married: single women tend to treat you as a confidant. In fifty seconds, going up in the lift with Alison today (first time we've spoken), she told me her mother had moved to Leeds; divorced her father five years ago; her father had married an American; divorced her and is living now with another woman. I got out at the third floor.

Other women in our wardrobe:

Gail – American, late twenties, bottle blonde, a quick tongue. She wears the flowery pyjama trousers poor women and gypsies wear. I must have made some remark: next time we met, she joined hands as in prayer, rolled up her eyes and murmured, "Mustn't mock The People's holy trousers."

I hardly know her. At the start of term, she took up with another American and spent most of her time in his flat, underneath Geoffrey's.

"What a knob hound," Geoffrey used to complain. "At it night, noon and morning."

Now Dave has gone back to the States, Gail is back in her flat and Geoffrey has peace again.

She has adopted a stray kitten she picked up in the street and brings it everywhere. I was standing at the door the other night when she brought it down to take the air.

"Any word from Dave?" I said.

"Who?" Puzzled look clearing slowly. "Oh, Dave! No. No … "

She introduced me to her kitten. It's called "Kedi".

Deirdre – Irish, thirtyish, white-framed glasses, moon face, miniskirt. One day in the staff room I was reading when she came up behind me and tapped me on the shoulder. I jumped.

"You *recoiled*!" she said. "Why do I have that effect on men?"

She has developed a crush on Murat Bey, the (as he says) gymnastic teacher, a past master at hand-springs, back-somersaults. Otherwise, as the Turks say, Murat Bey has hay in his head. But, apart from his forehead, perpetually knotted as if he is trying to solve some problem, he is extraordinarily handsome: skin like tin, bright black hair and moustache, delicate straight nose, a walk like a prince and an endless wardrobe. He appeared one day in cream duck trousers that everyone admired – except Deirdre.

"I'd prefer him without them," she sighed.

I haven't seen any men recoil from her (except Edmund: "A bit of a tart," he said disdainfully). In fact, when an American warship was here recently I saw her in a bar surrounded by a dozen sailors. "Did you see them?" she said to me next day. "Sitting around me *like lions*!"

Talking about something or other, I said, "I need an anchor."

Deirdre gave her film star sigh: "I need ships that pass in the night."

Helen – English, late fifties. She left last week and went down to Dubai looking for work. She never liked it here: "Like the set for a Cold War film." The night before going, she called to say goodbye and we sat chatting until late – we discovered we had both done a stint in the same part of Iran. Suddenly she started to cry. She hated leaving, she said. I said she didn't have to. "But I told you," she said, "I hate it here."

She offered me her reading-lamp, quite an expensive one. I said, "Are you sure you don't want it?"

"God, no." The weary decisive way she said it made me laugh – and she began to cry again. We promised to keep in touch.

Speaking of lamps: Tom was reminiscing in the minibus this morning about past girlfriends. " … Nice girl, Monika. Gave me a lamp once – 'Because you bring light in my life.' A bit funny like that … "

And Francesca: " … Lovely girl. Like slavery trying to talk with her though. 'You like Pet Shop Boys?' 'How many brothers you have?' That's one thing about Steph – you can have a bit of a conversation … "

(Oddly – I thought they'd have something in common – Tom and Edmund don't get on. Tom dropped down to visit him one evening. Verdict: "Gives me the creeps – the way he looks at you. Anyway, there has to be something wrong with someone who liked Morocco as much as he did."

Edmund: "That young *fellow* lives on his nerves.")

21 February 1988

Last pay-day, Irene was behind me as we queued into the school office to collect our envelopes and sign the register. I try not to look at what the Turkish teachers get, it's so embarrassing (of course I've noticed – about half our rate). But it wasn't until Irene said to me afterwards, "You're on the junior rate?" that I realised there is a double standard for native speakers as well. I've been getting what Grant and the other young teachers are getting, while Irene is on the higher scale. When Tom told me that he also gets the extra 100,000 liras a month, I decided to telephone Norbert's office. After some hand-over-mouthpiece delay, the secretary put me on to him.

"Hello-oo?" (Guarded, anonymous.)

I told him.

"You're getting what we agreed at the interview. You signed a contract, you know."

"I didn't know there were two scales. I've been teaching

English for ten years. Why am I on the beginner's scale?"
One advantage of getting old: you speak more directly; not
from greater courage, just less concern with others' reaction.

Instant retreat: "Why, why does everyone 'put legs' on
everything I do?"

His voice was so plaintive, I felt ashamed. "I ... " I
began retreating too.

"Adrian – " warm, intimate voice, " – why don't we have
lunch together and talk it over?"

"All right."

"Sunday? I'm always at home on Sunday."

So last Sunday I took the bus down to Bostanci and got
the ferry.

The Princes' Isles, Sea of Marmara ... The address on
Norbert's letter offering me a job had impressed me almost
as much as the string of degrees after his name. This wasn't
what I had expected. I'm used to it now. Apartment block
slabs on either side along the Asian and European shore.
The stink of sewage. We sailed down into the wider sea
where the *Lodos*, the wind blowing up from the Aegean all
winter, hit us, throwing the sea into waves, an army of
white horses thudding against the side of the boat as it made
south-east for the islands. ("Istanbul's weather" a passenger
translated a Turkish proverb, "is as fickle as its women.")

A tray level on the palm of his hand, a tilted waiter came
down the saloon chanting. "*Salep*" they call this steaming
gluey sweet milk crusted with ground cinnamon. I felt it,
first food of the day, going down my throat to my stomach,
fluttering nervous for some reason. Spray, thick and white
as my drink, rattled on the windows, melting the snow
there, both running down in streams across the deck and
overboard.

Why was I nervous? From thinking how I had landed
here. *Causality*, a word from Religious Knowledge class in
school popped up in my memory. A half-inch advertisement

noticed in a newspaper had brought me here. Another might as easily have brought me somewhere else. Where? Why? The islands appeared, blurs of cypress green and clay red. The pier was deserted except for two shivering white uniformed marines brushing icicles from their sub..achine gun barrels. The tourists had gone and the pretty horse carriages. Summer houses shuttered up, the island was just an island now: a man, with a tartan scarf wrapped about his head as a turban, driving a herd of farting goats up the empty village street, treading their steaming droppings into the snow; a woman in a snow-thatched hut milking – hissing steaming – a cow into an old olive oil drum; wind rattling through eucalyptus trees, whistling through sea pines.

"Greenhill" is the name of the house ("And it's *not* far away!" Dr Norbert likes to say) – a bungalow reached by steps cut into an almost vertically steep slope. When I knocked, there was no reply. Above the wind I heard a television loud inside. I waited for a lull in the volleys of canned laughter, then knocked harder. Silence. Rustling about. Then he appeared at the glass door, opened it – "Come in if you're good-looking!" – pressed it shut with his bottom against the gale. He has no hips, a boy's body, I noticed as he led the way inside.

The hall is a lean-to with a perspex roof painted green, throwing an underwater light. He switched on a lamp, but the shade is sky blue, turning everything an orange colour. ("I feel at *home*," Edmund said the night of Norbert's party. "It's like the kips.")

It's like everything. A brothel: red plush wallpaper, red lampshades in the sitting-room. A church: the half light, the large framed colour photograph of Pope John Paul leaning on his crucifix-topped staff. A home: cat curled up by the stove. A hotel: for everything somehow has that neat impersonal air. Fantastic too: a white rabbit was sitting by another stove contemplating the cat through half-closed pink eyes; a curtain of striped coloured plastic turned out to be a door of ribbons through which Dr Norbert disappeared. From there he called, "About the money – that's all right. You'll be on five-fifty thousand next month. Don't say anything to the others. Now – " his head appeared through the strips of red, blue, green, yellow, " – what would you like? 'Where are you at?' as they say. Breakfast? Lunch? 'Brunch'?"

There was a spiced stew he heated up and served on a tray, the knife and fork wrapped in a yellow paper napkin (orange in the red light). He sat on the other side of the room, short legs crossed to keep his tray level. I had been expecting a long argument about money and fumbled now for some other conversation. I mentioned having read that Trotsky stayed on this island with his daughter for a time, before his final flight to Mexico.

"Trotsky ... Trotsky," Norbert tapped fingertips on cheekbone.

"You know – Leon Trotsky. I wonder which house he lived in? I'd be interested to see."

"Ah! *Leon* Trotsky. Yes, I think we met ... "

I smiled, preparing to laugh, stopping at his glance: the look of someone instinctively aware he had made a mistake but wasn't sure what; who had been put down a thousand times before by smarter, bigger, richer or better educated people – and then one day had decided he wasn't taking any more. With an offhand smile, not quite masking the steel underneath, he added, "We must ask my houseboy, Barish – the name incidentally means 'Peace' – who should be along later."

A strange accent. I tried to analyse it as we made polite small talk: Irish vowels, elided English 'r's, all set in the varnish a language takes on after long separation from its native home. What was behind it? I wondered. Through the hairline crack of the Trotsky mistake, I glimpsed a vast, resentful sense of inferiority. That would explain the self-mocking clothes (tiger-striped kaftan today) and house decor. I abandoned this home-kit psychology as he poured the wine and glanced out the window at the pines and the pine green sea beyond, both slashed through with white. A blind man would have looked more interested: it was one hundred per cent indifference, unfeigned, unselfconscious, piercingly real. The hairline crack closed up. I felt I had touched solid ground, even as the small talk glided on.

"And how is Edmund getting on? I hear you two have 'hit it off'."

"He says he'd like to piss off to England." Suddenly I felt at ease, cosy, relaxed. Norbert was delighted, a tittering fellow conspirator.

"'Piss off to England'! Well, I won't – to coin a phrase – stand in his way. But who else would have him now? Got the shove from Morocco when he touched sixty, you know. 'Lord, to whom shall we go ... ' And Tom? Poor Tom?"

"Sober. Bored."

"It's depression, Adrian, that's all it is. I told him. 'Tom,' I said, *drink won't help*. You must face life ... ' And how is Irene? She seems more confident now, less shy, which is a good thing ... "

Was he serious? He seemed to be, but suddenly I was afraid I was going to burst out laughing. It was as if there was someone behind his back making faces at me. For a sweating minute I bit my lip. That under control, I was bored stiff. My attention drifted. I must have been looking at the portrait of the Pope.

"Old JP." Dr Norbert broke off his patter.

"Does he know you're here?"

"Oh yes, I'm attached to the Papal Nunciature here."

"Does that involve much – ?" 'Work' seemed the wrong word.

"No-ooo. They do 'their thing', I do mine." He smiled an Any More Questions smile, then – giving a scrap of meat to the cat, of potato to the rabbit – he took our trays out to the kitchen. His reading-glasses, on a string of glass beads, lay on a folded newspaper on a footstool. I had a sudden urge to see what he had been reading.

"Nescafé?" The toupee popped back through the coloured curtains.

Over the coffee and a plate of Milkchoc Goldgrain biscuits, he relaxed even more; legs crossed, one toe dangling a red-lined, black leather slipper. "You know, Adrian, people say to me, old friends from the seminary, when I'm back in Ireland, they say to me – 'What are the possibilities for evangelisation out there?' I tell them, '*Good example*, that's the true, the only way ... '"

"Irish seminary, was it?"

"More than one, Adrian, more than one. Yes, I was sent to school in Ireland, to a 'seminary', as they used to call them." He mentioned a religious house I had heard of, famous for its severe rule, chose another biscuit, licked genteely a chocolate smear from a fingertip. "I always remember the evening I arrived there, a young boy from home. You know: glimpses of furze through the mist, large stone buildings. And the *cold*! An old priest had just died and was laid out in the chapel. In his coffin. Without the lid, Adrian. And his nose – it was *blue* with cold. Oh dear, I thought, I don't think I'll be able for this."

"You stuck it out all the same."

"Not in that particular order." He took his coffee in a series of sips, as if denoting the passage of time. "But here I am. This is my home now. I am happy here. Here I shall end my days ... "

These augustan reflections were disturbed suddenly. One of the stoves had been giving off a smell of oil, and now flames began to stick their tongues out. The cat – or

72

rabbit, I forget which – bolted as Dr Norbert jumped up in a fluster, took an iron and lifted the hot plate. A red blaze shot up through black smoke and he cried, "Water! Get water!"

I remembered trying that once with a frying pan fire at home. I said, "That only scatters the flames."

"And WHAT?" All at once he seemed hysterically helpless, one hand pressed to the breast of his kaftan, the other holding the stove lid at arm's length.

"They say sand … or clay – "

He was outside with a fire shovel scraping snow off the minute garden. I found an empty biscuit tin and he filled it. Half would have done but he tippled it all down into the stove, composure returning as the fire went out. "Earth to earth," he intoned and as I laughed his eyes met mine – for an instant he was laughing too – then glanced away. He flapped a hand when I suggested clearing out the mass of clay and embers – "Barish will do that – " then glanced at his watch – "Ooh! Look, I have an appointment … No – " hand held up, " – stay as long as you like. Finish your coffee. Make yourself at home. There's 'Konyak' in the kitchen … " He put on shoes, an overcoat and then a black, priest's hat – what a hat! a 1950s high-crowned, curly brimmed, black-banded Anthony Eden – and vanished down the slope.

At once I began looking around. For what? For "clues", I suppose. The folded up paper was the *News of the World*. There was a video recorder with a stack of tapes underneath. I went through them one by one. What was I expecting? Pornography? Their ordinariness surprised me even more: *Postman Pat … Grease … Carry on at your Convenience … Mountbatten – The Final Years*. In a rising line like china ducks on the red plush wallpaper hung a row of tiny gilt-framed masterpieces: *Mona Lisa … Laughing Cavalier … Monarch of the Glen*. A stack of records: Cilla Black ... Trini Lopez ... Body 'n' Soul. A shelf of books and airport paperbacks: Bible ... *Colditz – The Inside Story ... Shakespeare ... Confessions of a Window Cleaner*.

I looked into the bedroom: an alarm clock galloping in the silence; neat white counterpaned bed, a horoscope magazine, *Your Stars for May*, on a spotlessly bare bedside table. And suddenly I felt soiled, a dirty Nosey Parker; and worse, I felt that Norbert had known what I would do, knew what I had done. His sudden departure, so natural-seeming, was deliberate. Why else, I thought, would he have walked out into the snow. He had deliberately left me on my own ... "Go on, look for yourself!" I imagined him saying as I put on my coat – my eyes still wandering around the sitting-room. There was a letter on the sideboard. I almost ran to pick it up: a typed note from a Yorkshire local government authority answering some query about social security. "You won't believe, will you?" the voice seemed to say. "You can't believe it's as simple as this. There's nothing else. *Nothing*. But go on, look."

I dithered as I went out the door. Should I lock it after me? Had he a key? Again I imagined Norbert somewhere smiling at my confusion. I left it an inch ajar, but halfway down the slope I turned back and put the lock on the snib, then drew it shut.

28 February 1988

I forgot to mention Marjorie. English. Fortyish. She's married to Peter, who left the police force to study theology. Now, for some reason, they're here teaching. They're from Ross-on-Wye – "Five minutes and we're in the woods!" Marjorie says. She never calls a tree a tree, but uses the proper name: "Over there, by the oak," when she's pointing out the bus stop. She writes letters to the *Turkish Daily News* protesting at the way animals are treated in Istanbul zoo. (The poor wolf there is pelted with stones by visiting countrymen.) She's also had an article published: "Turkey – Whither?"

Every week they put up a notice on the board inviting all to their Bible study group. Their flat is next to Gail's, who was with Dave the night I went last Christmas.

"And is it true? And is it true … ?" Peter's reading of John Betjeman's poem on the Nativity was ruined by the rattle of the bed and Gail's cries next door. That wasn't commented on, but Marjorie's fury was let loose later when the poor *Boza* man came down the street selling his ware, a kind of drink made from fermented millet, which is said to help sleep.

"*Bo-za!*" Loud like an opera singer before he even appears on stage. Marjorie went to the window and watched him crawl around the corner, his back bent under his tin keg. "*Bo-zaaa!*"

"Of course he doesn't care *whom* he disturbs!" She led us all then in a terrific singing of *Good King Wenceslas*.

William, a pale-faced young Ulster Protestant, is the only regular. With a Bible as heavy-looking as the *Boza* man's keg, he comes up the stairs to make "a two or three gathered in His name," as he puts it.

I didn't go back a second time. After the Christmas carols, Marjorie complained about this year's midnight service in St George's church being cancelled.

"You could always go to midnight Mass in Kadiköy," I ventured.

"I don't want to go to midnight Mass, thank you very much. I want to go to the *Consulate*."

They have made one concession to the Mediterranean: they go to an Italian restaurant every Sunday after church. "Non-Turkish, that's the main thing," Marjorie says. "The lavatory is so clean, you could eat your dinner off the floor."

Inci invited her to a Lions' Club meeting recently where Marjorie got a lot off her chest. "Look at the roads, the footpaths, the telephone wires all tangled up hanging a few feet off the ground … " She was warming up in the hall while she waited for Inci to collect her. "Why can't they *do* something?"

13 March 1988

Sunday. Tom and myself were chatting with Deirdre outside the hall door this morning when Inci drove up to collect her. They had organised a picnic and we went along too. Spring is here – a warm sun in a bare sky. (Down in Florya woods last Sunday the bluebells were out in drifts, and the first families, and the gypsies busking through the trees with flutes and drums.) Car windows rolled down and a breeze flapping our sleeves, we drove down the western highway, then turned off at the Bosphorous shore road; Nat King Cole crooning on the cassette player. Inci tapes all the English-language programmes. Sometimes they overlap:

"Are you warm, are you real, Mona Lisa, or just a cold and perfect work of art … ? In the House of Commons today Mrs Thatcher said … "

We stopped at some ruined Ottoman timber mansion by the sea where they had arranged to meet the rest of the party, including Deirdre's latest boyfriend. I was curious to see what he was like. "I'm in love … " she had breathed a few weeks before, sitting down opposite me in the staffroom. "Don't tell old drippy drawers" – she can't stand Irene. "His name's Faisal. Like the king!"

"What's he like?"

"Gorgeous. Lovely long fingers. Into nature and all that. I told him I was twenty-nine – no harm to knock a few years off. He's the manager in a car factory. Pucks of dough."

There was no one about the old house except a fisherman. We bought half a dozen *palamut* from him and then, leaving Tom and me to meet the others, Deirdre and Inci went off to buy wine. We must have been waiting half an hour, wandering through the ruined mansion – room after grandly proportioned room stripped bare as if by a vacuum cleaner, except for one, violently pornographic, magazine page nibbled to lace by mice. We were, I'm ashamed to say, trying to piece it together when a car horn blared below.

Balding, at least as old as Deirdre, Faisal's only apparent attraction was his scent of money, as powerfully sweet as the *Poison* perfume Deirdre drenches herself with. They had met in the Hilton Bar, he said; he spoke excellent English and chatted with Tom while we waited, discussing the correct temperature at which Guinness should be served.

Edmund has his way of spending his money, Deirdre has hers. "Now, a taxi to Taksim," she says on pay day and off she goes, coming back in the night with a Benetton bag or two, and stories of film producers or American army officers she has met. Searching her handbag for one of these bigwigs' cards one night, she pulled out a packet of contraceptives by mistake, said, "Ten thousand liras! But it's worth it – you never know, do you?" and dropped it back again.

"Faisal, darling!" To my ears at least she sounded like someone making an entry on the Abbey stage. She waltzed to meet him, throwing her pancake make-up cheek sideways to be kissed.

"Hello, Dede!" Faisal embraced her with the long fingers.

"Deir-dreh! Think of 'Dear'!" She rolled her eyes at me over his shoulder.

While shopping, they had met Inci's friend, Omer, who was to bring us to the picnic place, so off we went up the

Bosphorous hills in convoy. This is the place to live in Istanbul. In the *Daily News* column of houses for sale, the "O" section is longest, so many advertisements begin "On the Bosphorous – ." Here live the diplomats, those gypsies with dinner jackets, their encampments marked by flags. Above live the rich, in villas balanced on rock ledges, hermits contemplating the mystery of money. We climbed higher up a steep country road, turned down a narrower road through green woodland. We must have driven a mile before I noticed barbed wire fencing, designer green, along one side of the road. Omer's car signalled and we followed as he turned in an entrance guarded by armed soldiers. His father, Inci explained, was an officer and this fenced-in forest was one of the many rewards the army had given itself. The guards joked with Omer, then swung open a spike-topped gate and we drove up a sand road into a fairyland of sap green light.

"Wouldn't you know Faisal'd pick a place like this." Clearly, this wasn't what Deirdre had been expecting. The noise of birdsong was deafening. Saplings grew up through the branches of long fallen trees. Purple weeds were thick as wheat on either side of the track. She brightened up as the cars ahead stopped outside a timber cottage where other friends of Omer's sat about in the sun drinking and smoking.

Omer, Inci explained, was "crazy". About thirty, with a sixteen-year-old's smile, he didn't work but lived all the year here, caretaking his family's summer house. Despite the Lions Club badge on his windcheater, he didn't speak a word of English. Smiling, hopping from one foot to the other, he began introducing his friends.

"Musa – "

Musa, a broad young man with a moustache (one of those big black Turkish moustaches which make you think of diguises) took over, jumping up to shake hands all round and then introducing his friend – "Frederic – "

Frederic told us, in English so perfect it was hard to believe, that he was Dutch.

"Dutch? How exciting!" Deirdre trilled. "What are you doing here?"

Frederic smiled lazily, introducing the girl sitting beside him – "This is Esra," and added, "we are artists."

"Artists!" Deirdre's doubts about the day disappeared. In a few minutes she was sipping a glass of wine, waving one of her Dunhill cigarettes about and ascending into her Hilton Bar world.

I was a bit peeved. Recently, by colossal fluke, Geoffrey had found a book with some stories of mine in the British Council library and had passed it about. A few days later Deirdre said to me, "I read your stories," in the voice people say "I saw the death in the paper," and then gently changed the subject. So I joined Inci, who was gutting the fish into a sheet of newspaper, the talk as usual turning to my family. How were they? Was I not lonely? I've grown used to this conversation: every month Mr Seyid, the bank manager, asks me the same question, looking at me like a doctor presented with a strange case. ("Same in Saudi," Geoffrey commented. "Everything's family – and bloody boring. Yes, as far as I'm concerned, the Turk's just an Arab in trousers.") Wearying of this, I asked Inci about herself and learned that, like several of the Turkish women in our school, she is divorced. Married at seventeen – "In Turkey it is so, I think it is rubbish," – she has been living alone for ten years now.

"What happened?"

"Nothing! Nothing ever happen and so I – " she made a cut with the bloody knife – "I go! Now I am OK!"

"You're like me," Deirdre drifted over to us, " – a survivor."

"Survivor?" Inci was upset at not knowing this word.

"You explain," Deirdre said to me. "You're the writer."

Still peeved, I said, "Someone who's hard."

"What do you want me to be?" Deirdre said. "A big baby?"

"Hard?" Inci frowned. "No, I am not hard."

"Wait till you've been on the road ten years." Deirdre gave her film star sigh.

"'On the road'," Tom mimicked. "Jesus, you're an English teacher, not a gypsy."

"Gypsy?" Inci said. "*Çingene?*"

Deirdre sighed again, glancing across at Faisal and, following her glance, I saw why she had joined us. Faisal was laughing and talking in Turkish with Esra and Frederic. She turned reluctantly back to us, talking loudly to show she wasn't being left out. "I was hitching once, trying to make a town before dark and the rain was teeming down. Well, it got darker and heavier and I was still walking when this gypsy cart came rattling along and I said – Damn it, I don't care how I travel, *I'll get there*. So I put my thumb out and do you know what? They just looked at me, dripping wet in the dark in the middle of nowhere and – they just laughed! and drove past. Now *that's* hard."

"They're survivors," I said.

"I'm not complaining. They taught me to look after myself better next time."

"It is not very nice," Inci said.

"It's what happens. Religion and all that – they don't survive when you're travelling. I mean, the gypsies – they don't go to the mosque, do they?"

"*Çingene* go to *Cami*? No! Never!" Inci smiled her sad, gold-toothed smile. "Now they are all going to Edirne. Every year they have big kermesse there."

"*Kermesse?*" I said. "How did that word get into Turkish?"

"Words travel too," Frederic said, turning to join our conversation. But this made Deirdre only more annoyed, for

80

now Faisal was giving attention undivided to Esra.

"We're all travellers now." Deirdre rolled her eyes dreamily behind her big white-framed glasses.

"In what way?" Frederic said dryly.

I needn't have worried about Deirdre. She seemed able to look after herself: "I'm Irish, you're Dutch, Inci comes from Thrace. Every kid in the school tells me his father comes from somewhere in Anatolia. Why do you think they're building these tower blocks by the thousand?"

"Because people are settling down?"

This interesting conversation was interrupted by loud sudden laughter from Faisal. Esra slapped one hand off the other and cried "Aie!" in delight, then called something in Turkish to Inci, who explained that the two of them had just discovered they came from the same village. Mentioning names, laughing even more, they led the way into the kitchen to make the dinner.

"Aie my eye," Deirdre muttered to me.

Omer stood watching in fascination as his chalet was turned upside down; jumping each time someone asked him where something was, running into the next room to fetch another chair, vanishing outside and returning with a sprig of basil. While we watched the fish fry in a basin-sized pan of olive oil, Faisal and Esra explained that they had not met since they were children. Since then, like Inci, Esra had married and divorced. Like Frederic – they shared a studio in Istanbul – she was a painter. Every few minutes she and Faisal would look at each other, laugh aloud again and slap each other on the back. Tall, dark-haired, her face blotched from smoking cigarettes, she was not very handsome – but so lively she was the centre of attention all through dinner.

How the Turks love fish. Smoked eel – "I would eat my father if he came from the sea." Faisal quoted a Turkish proverb. Then the *palamut* – "tunnies steep'd in brine ... ": Tom, steeped in wine, slurred a verse of *The Scholar Gypsy*, stopping short as the raki and ice appeared. Then the music

81

began. Soon Esra was dancing with Omer – his face staring wide-eyed at us above her head as she waltzed him about the small wooden room. A Turkish tape next and she and Faisal retreated, advanced on each other, gazing grave into each other's faces; standing tiptoe, hands outspread, fingers clicking.

"A bit of a show-off, isn't she?" Deirdre watched sullenly. Esra was a natural dancer, her body rippling with the music right to her fingertips; breasts, hips, stomach warming to the rhythm. The sound of birdsong broke in from outside, was cut off again as Omer ran to put on another tape – Western rock this time. Deirdre asked Frederic to dance and soon they were jiving, Esra and Faisal standing back, clapping hands, laughing as a slow Beatles song took Deirdre into Frederic's arms and they did a cheek-to-cheek glide.

"Wasting my time," Deirdre said in my ear as she sat down again.

"You seemed to be doing all right."

"He's gay. I should've known – an artist." She looked at me in disgust, as if I was partly to blame.

I didn't hear how she had found out, for now Esra was calling me out onto the timber floor. Esra had the authority of party queen, summoning and dismissing partners. After twenty minutes of furious dancing and conversation about the Impressionists shouted above the music, I was replaced by Faisal and I sat down again. Now Deirdre was talking with Musa, her plump Bodrum-tanned legs crossed, pulling her white miniskirt down on her thighs as regularly as she sipped her raki, waving a gold-banded Dunhill.

Tom, sitting at the table still, a raised glass propped against his lower lip.

"What are you thinking of?" I said. "Stephanie?"

Tom: "I was wondering – if I put down this glass, will I be able to lift it up again?"

Frederic turned to me with a smile: "I have never been

82

to Ireland."

I said I had never been to Holland. From that we moved on to explain why we were in Turkey. My explanation didn't take long. Frederic – latish twenties, flat blond hair – had come here to paint because Turkey had no tradition of painting. I had noticed that, I said, in the commercial galleries along Istiklal Caddesi.

"Yes, they are dreadful. But for me, coming from Holland, this is refreshing."

"Do you not find Rembrandt and Van Gogh refreshing?"

"And then Rubens and Ruisdael and van Eyck and Vermeer and van Dyck … No, I find it oppressive. For over a thousand years Islam has forbidden images in the mosque and so, inevitably, discouraged them everywhere else. A painter here might learn to see life through his own eyes, not through art."

"But good art does just that. A good artist sees things with his own eyes."

"But we have had so many. It is like language. After a time it is worn into paths. And the artist, even the good artist, reacts by simply beating out yet another path."

"But isn't that all art is," I said, "a path? And the more paths we have, the more we learn about life?"

"No, art is life."

"Does that mean life is art?"

"Yes, there is no difference." Frederic, as if holding this sentence up to the light to consider a grammatical flaw, turned to gaze out the window. I turned to where Deirdre had been sitting, noticed that not only she but Musa also was missing.

"No, it is the same … " Frederic resumed, pausing and frowning again at this construction; smiling then as Esra sat down beside us, breathless. She filled a glass with ice, poured in the raki. At once the centre of gravity changed – Faisal almost shoving Omer to get the chair next to Esra.

But off the dance floor she was dull. Joining our floundering conversation, she sank it completely with some remarks of civil service banality: "We in Turkey will solve our artistic problems in our own way ... "

I was trying to fill the silence this made, asking where in Istanbul she and Frederic had their studio, when Faisal interrupted – "Where is Dede?"

"Musa – " Omer began. Faisal got up abruptly, went to the door and looked outside, then shouted. Omer, as if a game of hide and seek had begun, bounded out after him.

Evening had set in, the birdsong had ended. In the silence we heard Faisal's voice echoing through the wood – "Dede! Musa!" Omer ran back inside, all ready to organise a search party, looking disappointed as the bedroom door opened and Musa appeared. It clicked with me only as Frederic sprang up, beating even Faisal to it, saying something in Turkish as fluent as his English. Musa muttered something in reply as he crossed the room to the toilet, buttoning his shirt as casually as he could. Faisal blocked his way, speaking in a low hiss, glaring into his face so intently he did not see Deirdre come out of the bedroom – her white miniskirt crooked, a smudge like a skid-mark on her make-up, giving her smiling face a wild distortion.

"I think I straightened him out all right," she murmured to me, as Esra and Inci busied themselves silently in clearing the table.

Tom, oblivious, swaying about the room with a small round tin of something marked "Tiger Balm", smearing it on everyone's forehead (including his own), intoning in a priestly voice, "It develops the third eye ... "

I went for a walk in the woods, the dark alive with birdsong; not the shrill of the day, but a liquid music – nightingales, the first I have heard in over twenty years.

15 March 1988

"I imagine, though I do not know for certain, that Darius's bridge was halfway between Byzantium and the temple which stands on the strait between the Bosphorous and the Black Sea.

Darius was so pleased with the bridge that he loaded its designer with presents, and Mandrocles spent a certain portion of what he received in having a picture painted, showing the whole process of the bridging of the strait, and Darius himself sitting on his throne, with the army crossing over. This picture he presented as a dedicatory offering to the Temple of Hera, with the following verses inscribed upon it, to serve as a permanent record of his achievement:

Goddess, accept this gift from Mandrocles,
Who bridged the Bosphorous' fish-haunted seas.
His labour, praised by King Darius, won
Honour for Samos, for himself a crown."
(Herodotus: *The Histories*)

16 March 1988

Grant's girlfriend arrived from Australia last night. To my surprise, she's just as he described – open, simple. He introduced her this morning, told me they were going away for a week's holiday and then asked me would I give a "sickie" to the headmaster. He has it all worked out: the note is from a Turkish doctor, excusing him from work for a week (spring hayfever); plane tickets bought. They're going down to Bodrum.

18 March 1988

All around the city walls, plaques commemorate its capture in 1453. One of Sultan Mehmet Fatih's guns still stands outside Edirne Kapi. Is this the great cannon made by the Hungarian engineer Urban? Brought from Edirne by 60 oxen and 200 soldiers, when first fired at the walls it brought the citizens running out into the streets crying to God in terror. Each ball weighed 12 hundredweight. The gun could be fired seven times a day.

19 March 1988

Just how drunk does Tom get? In the minibus this morning he began chatting like Rip Van Winkle about last week's picnic party: "Was there something funny going on?"
 "There was."
 "I didn't break anything?"
 "Not you."
 "Funny. Thought I remembered something breaking … "
Yawns, sits up as the traffic moves on again.

20 March 1988

Hulya arrived into class this morning wearing a neck chain of pure gold, a present from her father for having read the entire Koran. She said it took her "ages".

23 March 1988

It would be nice to be just the detached spectator. Or would it? You'd have to be dead to be that. Anyway – my father, like Tom's, is dead. Like Irene, I have a mother two thousand miles away; like Geoffrey, a wife. We're just drawers in the same wardrobe. Tom is up in Stephanie's now, cooking one of his four star hotel dinners. I'm in mine, sitting before this rattling god. Three hours work for half a page. More and more, it seems to me, my writing is just a grown-up version of the exhausting hobbies I had as a boy: gathering birds' eggs and butterflies, identifying, contemplating, arranging them in drawers. Exactly the same, I thought this evening as I dropped off and my forehead banged down on the typewriter: once when I was putting a butterfly in the killing-bottle, I inhaled the chloroform myself and keeled over.

27 March 1988

Going to school this morning, the traffic was so bad that even west of the Bosphorous bridge we were stuck in a suffocating tail-back; crawling for a full hour behind a Coca-Cola lorry twenty yards long, its tarpaulin stamped all over "Sarajevo", its exhaust pipe puffing out Coke-coloured clouds of diesel smoke. This stretch of road we usually speed along at sixty miles an hour. Today I passed the time watching the sights in slow motion: a barefoot, pyjama-trousered woman out on a sill six floors up the Webster Dictionary block cleaning the window – a women inside gesturing her to clean the endmost panes; the crank cyclist; gypsy women with sickles, harvesting dead grass along the roadside; a wretched brown sheep tied to the bumper of a wrecked car, a pathetic "*satilik*" sign offering both for sale. Women who had left their doormats on the *asfalti* to be hammered clean by traffic wheels – nothing goes astray in Turkey – returned and took them home again.

Past the statue of Sultan Mehmet Fatih on his rearing horse, his hand waving like a furious traffic policeman. Then the *Tünel*, a quarter-mile long concrete pipe funnelling us under another motorway. Ragged boys stood at its blocked mouth, waist deep in carbon monoxide, selling bread rings, provisions for the underworld.

I noticed that in most cars the drivers, instead of reaching for the brown *fiche* envelope on the dashboard as usual, sat silent listening to their radios; and in the buses, usually like travelling dormitories, even the seated passengers were awake, talking to each other. Yet it wasn't until Tom woke up in the back seat, stretched and looked about and said, "What's up, Ali?" that the Turkish teachers realised we didn't know and told us. There had been a mass escape from "our" prison, Metris.

It was ten o'clock, we had missed our first class (Irene's eyes were sparkling) when we reached the pot-holed military road. The soldiers were everywhere, in couples, searching each car and minibus. Officers were actually running. Police by the score were holding back a sheepish crowd of journalists and a TV crew. Up on the prison roof more soldiers were walking about, small and black as jackdaws. A helicopter was quartering the shantytown in falcon sweeps. Tanks had been moved into positions at each corner of the prison wall. The guards were up in the searchlight towers at each end of the compound's barbed wire, practising swivels with the machine guns.

School was humming like a beehive disturbed. The headmaster never even mentioned our being late. In fact, though an old soldier, he smiled and said in his one-year-in-Fort-Bragg American accent, "Hey, I hear the prison governor is in prison!"

It was impossible to get the children to work. From the classroom window we could see coachloads of blue beret commandos arrive. Two of them dug in behind the school gate-piers. The children had heard the news at breakfast time, and so instead of English lessons we compromised: they explained what had happened – in English.

Twenty-nine prisoners – revolutionary peasant party, Kurdish separatists, militant communists – all due to be hanged next month, were discovered missing at morning check. Somehow, for the past six months (i.e. since we arrived) they had been digging a tunnel from the prison yard into a sewer which runs deep underground beneath the prison wall, compound and barbed wire, coming out into a moat which surrounds the whole place. From our window we could see the mouth of this drain where a soldier stood with rifle at the ready, a definitive groom bolting the stable door. It was thought the prisoners had taken pieces of metal from their bedframes and at night used them as trowels, digging when they were thought to be sleeping. How did they get out of their cells at night? I asked. No one knew. However, last night all twenty-nine, the cream of Turkey's political prisoners, walked out of Turkey's showcase prison and disappeared. The children were full of the radio's or their parents' or their own views: "These men hate Ataturk. They are fascists. They want to bring back the empire and destroy our constitution."

Life went on as usual otherwise. The porter got his bucket and facecloth and washed down Ataturk's bronze face in the yard.

28 March 1988

Again this morning everyone was awake in the buses, newspapers in hands. Even the English language *Daily News* had a full page about it: twenty-nine photographs with biographical details of the escaped men – a strange harsh note in its usual bland roundup of ex-pat. news (Princess Di's latest appearance, baseball results). Although you can turn up interesting information in the *Daily News*. Today, for instance, they published a morale-boosting list of Turkish businessmen paying international class income tax: seventh from the top comes a gentleman handing over 72,000,000 liras to the government; under the heading

"Occupation" – the frank "Brothel Owner."

From one of these newspaper pages of photographs the army has made photocopies and handed them out to the soldiers. Blurred black and white, soon creased from folding and unfolding, thumb-smudged – they could be of anyone. They made me nervous. Not Tom: "Talk about Spot the Ball," he said as we were stopped at the school gates and, fingers on triggers of rapid fire rifles, two commandos looked in our minibus window, then down at their photocopy sheets.

"Ben and Mandy went to the disco. They helped Mum at the supermarket and Dad gave them fifty p each ... " At the start of term these colour-photo strip-cartoon textbooks were wonderful to the children. Six months on they have become as dull as Latin grammars and the children almost sob with boredom taking them out in the morning. Now the escape has come to help me. Boys who never opened their mouths stand up and stammer an opinion in English. A statement has been published by Turkish dissidents in Holland saying that all the prisoners are safely abroad; Cem stood up from the back of the class and managed an English sentence telling us that his father works as a welder in Leyden.

Suddenly as familiar as "Hello" and "OK", the new English words – "Escape", "Free", – are flying about the school.

1 April 1988

Tom in the bus this morning: "Well, Irene, where did you go for the weekend?"

Irene: "*Hmm!* You'll want to know what I had for breakfast next."

Not so Grant. He returned from Bodrum last night – a week late – telling us all about it on the way to school. In

90

school he collected his pay and then gave notice. He has the knack of not noting anyone else's point of view. The headmaster recovered enough to ask when he was leaving and Grant looked at his watch and said, "In about ten minutes."

The Turkish teachers, so afraid of losing their jobs that they turn up even when they are dying of flu, looked on in disbelief. When the headmaster said awkwardly "I don't understand," Grant explained, as if to a slow pupil, that he had to see a travel agent. He and his girlfriend are going to London where Grant is resuming his career as a musician. When he turned his steady sincere smile on me and said "Goodbye, Adrian," I found myself smiling back, saying, "Goodbye, Grant."

Tom was the only one who spoke up: "You're a user, that's all you are."

Grant – sincere smile turning sad: "I'm afraid I don't see it like that."

Tom: "Bloody sure you don't."

Grant, calmly: "Cool it, Tom."

Tom: "Yeah, you're cool as fucking ice."

The Turkish teachers hissed in their breath with shock. Grant shook hands sincerely with the headmaster, who seemed suddenly flattered. Putting a hand on Grant's shoulder, he walked with him to the door, looking back with a glare at Tom.

2-3 April 1988

Full Spring. I went to Iznik (old Nicaea) about forty miles east for the weekend. Fields of blue cabbage. Vines pruned back to the ground sprouting green. Row on row of olive trees wheeling from grey-green to silver before the breeze. Yoked pairs of oxen ploughing the earth underneath. Women working furiously, gathering dead weeds and piling them on small fires that blaze everywhere, bright as their clothes. Beyond the smoke – a dark range of mountains where the snow still lies in magpie patches. An eagle on a telegraph pole. Police roadblocks everywhere.

The First Oecumenical Council met here in 325 AD by order of the Emperor Constantine. This pagan Christian king regarded the Church as his predecessors regarded the Imperial Cult – as his own religion; saw differences of belief as a threat to the unity of his empire – hence his calling a council where his bishops should formulate a creed binding all. But that need not decrease the value of the Nicene Creed any more than, say, the Fourth Crusade. From that Christian terror the Emperor Theodore withdrew here a thousand years later, and from here his successor, Michael, recaptured Constantinople, so quickly and with such surprise that the western King Baldwin was in bed when they arrived; he had time just to dress and slip down from Blanchernae Palace to a getaway ship, leaving even his crown and sceptre behind.

From here too the Ottoman Turks launched their attack on Constantinople, a longer, less surprising affair; but if the emperor died fighting, his noblemen had different ambitions. A passenger list survives from that day, 29 May 1453, with the names of those leaving on a Genoese ship: Cantacuzene, Palaeologos, Lascarid, Komneni, Notaros ... a constellation of the past centuries' ruling families, united at last in flight. The Cardinal Isidore, too, showed himself wiser than the children of light: as he fled, he met a beggar and offered to swap his red robe for the rags; the gorgeous beggar was executed by the conquering Turks.*

---

* Possibly with the same motive, what Gibbon calls "prudent despair", Constantine Palaeologus, the last Roman emperor, cast off his purple cloak – only to be killed in the general massacre; his corpse, found under a heap of slain, was later identified by the golden eagles embroidered on the shoes.

Nicaea now is a quiet market town: old tractors putt-putting along the cobbled Roman grid streets; instead of bloody corpses, heaps of rotting tomatoes lie under the city walls; goats filing under Hadrian's triumphal arch. The church where the mystery of the Trinity was defined is in ruins except for a tower topped by a stork's nest big enough to hold a dozen bishops.

There is a near magic feeling, like finding you can swim, when you start to speak a foreign language; when the ragbag collection of words joins with verbs and suddenly you are speaking in sentences. When I was here last autumn I had an exhausting mime conversation with a dealer who invited me into his shop. This afternoon, I was hardly half an hour in the town when he had found me again, remembered my name, picked me up in his claws and carried me back to his magpie's nest of old coins and clay fragments.

Ibrahim is an antique dealer, but since most of that is illegal, he has a façade of rugs and leather belts he can finger while he does his real business. A master salesman, his manner is complete, leisurely indifference. In fact, I think he is indifferent whether I buy or not. He's old, has made his money long ago, but still likes the business of doing business. Admiring a cow going by, he asked the English word for the turquoise beads decorating her forehead, then told me the Turkish – *firuz*; asked how much money she would fetch in Ireland, told me how much she would fetch here – an awful lot, £600. My Turkish flattered, he slipped a few ancient bronze coins from his breast pocket and passed them to me without a word: idealised Hellenic profiles of feminine-looking men and masculine-looking women, blurred over by a patina of green. How much? When he told me and I handed them back, he slipped them behind his breast pocket handkerchief.

A country boy arrived with some coins he had found.

With the same leisurely indifference, Ibrahim unknotted the dirty handkerchief and spilled the hoard into his hand: a Deutsche Mark and some pfennigs. As if refusing a nice offer, he tilted back his head, returned the bundle to the boy with a smile, then turned back to me. A tiny terracotta head this time – he produced it from nowhere – the features worn into an ethereally characterless smile. I couldn't resist. Ibrahim did not see my wallet as I took out money to pay, yet knew somehow exactly how much I had to spare. A broken Roman oil lamp, the clay still smoke-blackened ... a coin, very worn, with *Herakles Soter*, Herakles the Saviour, just legible about the rim. I fell, fell again. Subtracting the cost of my bed and breakfast and my boat fare back to Istanbul, I had only two thousand liras left. Apologetically, Ibrahim produced a copy of an ancient clay lamp, pointing out with an old man's *hors de combat* smile the design – a man making love to a woman from behind. I had an attack of desire. "How much?" I asked.

"Two thousand liras," Ibrahim said – his only, small mistake. I hadn't known he could speak English.

Back in Istanbul this evening, on the bus home, I met Marion. We have hardly spoken in six months. Her flat is several floors above mine and we teach in different schools. She's Irish, about my age, and keeps to herself. Teaching abroad for the past twenty years, she still has a piercingly pure Kerry accent.

"Yerra, I was back in Istiklal Caddesi." She goes to Mass there every Sunday afternoon. I asked her did she go home much.

"To the local pothole, is it?"

A strong unhappy face. I told her I was on the third floor, next door to Edmund. She said that she knew him from Morocco; they had been teaching in the same town.

"Loved talking, always talking. 'Is there a God?' and

'What is Free Will?' Sure, he'd open your head."

And: "I suppose he was telling you about Houriah? She wasn't much looking indeed."

And: "Always in the cafés talking. There was only one time ever he shut up. Some young fella came out from England to stay with him. Well, we didn't see Edmund for weeks."

"Who was he?" I asked.

"They were saying he was Edmund's son. Sure, you wouldn't know … "

5 April 1988

One of the escaped prisoners was recaptured – in Istanbul. He went home for a change of clothes and his father turned him in.

6 April 1988

" … We accept as being probably enough, the story told by Ridolfi, that the Sultan on being presented by Gentile Bellini with a picture of the head of John the Baptist on a charger, remarked that he had made the adhering portion of the neck project from the head, which was incorrect, as it always retired close to the head when this was separated from the body. To prove he was correct, the Sultan had the head of a slave cut off and demonstrated the truth of what he said there and then. Such was the man who was the indirect cause of the revival of classic literature in Western Europe … "

(Forbes Robertson's *The Great Painters of Christendom*.)

In class today the word "shepherd" cropped up. I tried everything – bleating like a sheep, drawing a crooked staff on the blackboard. Blank faces, until *Çigdem* suddenly understood and turning to the others mimed playing a flute. Everyone, at once: "Ah! *Çoban*."

Çigdem is a scholarship girl, her father is "*head* waiter" in a restaurant. She tells me that someone ("Not Turkish; a foreigner, *yabanci*") with AIDS dined there recently. When her father found out, he smashed everything that had been on the table: glasses, plates, cups, saucers; threw out the knives and forks and spoons, burned the tablecloth.

7 April 1988

Pay day – a week late, but Norbert was as good as his word and I got 550,000 liras.

Edmund: "I'm afraid I fell by the *wayside* again … "

The girl knew one word of English, "saxophone". I said it didn't seem like much of a prelude to love-making and he told me that she said one other word, "kaput".

"I thought she was trying to tell me I was past it. It turned out she meant "*capote*". I don't usually wear one, Adrian. I don't like them. Anyhow, I didn't *rise* to the occasion."

"I'm sorry, Edmund."

"No, no – there are other ways of enjoying yourself. I kissed her from head to toe … well almost."

Apparently, he always asks the girl to keep her shoes on, preferably black sling-back high heels. He's down to the bottom of his bottle of *Altin* now, swallowing mouthfuls of gold dust.

I asked him if he remembered Marion in Morocco.
Edmund: "That *nun*?"

10 April 1988

Serdar Bey is a devout follower of the Ataturk cult. Besides the death mask on his desk (it's eerie to watch him fiddle with it as he talks to someone on the telephone), he has photographs of the hero all about his office. Now he is painting a portrait. Snapshot in one hand (it shows Ataturk in white tie and evening coat), paintbrush in the other, he lunges from palette to canvas. It must be seven foot high. If energy could bring Ataturk back to life, he would have stepped forth by now, tangerine-faced, colossal, into Serdar's office. Tom and I were passing the door this afternoon and he called us in to ask our opinion, raising a moustache-sized eyebrow and gesturing to the easel. It is the worst painting I have ever seen, an illustration in fact of everything Frederic said about Turkish art at that picnic party.

Coward to the last, I gave a thumbs-up sign. Tom said, "Looks a bit like Norbert." (And it's true – the hair laid on like a toupee, the black coat, did suggest the reverend father.) Luckily Serdar Bey doesn't know a word of English. Unluckily, Murat Bey, the gym teacher, was there too and, as I hurried Tom away, I heard him translate exactly what had been said.

"He's getting very good at English," I remarked.

"Why wouldn't he?" Tom said. "Isn't he going out with Irene."

I was amazed, asked how he knew.

"Amn't I across the corridor from her? I saw him slipping in the other night."

As usual when you hear something, you see it for yourself soon after. I was going out for a drink this evening when I saw Murat Bey getting into the lift, self-conscious with a small gift-wrapped parcel, the gold ribbon teased into a knot the size of a chrysanthemum, the collar of his snazzy black leather jacket turned up about his face.

And as usual in this tower block, news carries like the cooking smells. When I got back, Deirdre had heard.

Drunk, she knocked at my door, came in and began to cry, tears running off her pancake make-up like raindrops down fresh paint.

"The little bitch. And she knew I liked him. I told her I liked him."

"Why did you?" I tried to think of something sympathetic to say.

"She told me she had this fella at home. 'But I can't rely on him … '" She took off Irene's voice. "Of course, that's why she's here. She'd never get a fella at home – the miserable dull little N.T … Ah well, I suppose it's because she knows the bit of Turkish … " She dried her eyes, put on her glasses and went back to her flat. But out in the corridor she met Gail and I heard her telling the whole story again, crying again, her voice ringing off the walls – "The little bitch … of course she's hard as nails, the bitch, the little fucking sneaky bitch … "

CHAPTER SIX

1 May 1988

PAY DAY, AND AS USUAL I GOT OFF THE MINIBUS AS IT SKIRTED THE
city walls and made the rest of the way on foot. This
monthly walk ends at the Yapi Kredit bank where Mr Seyid
the manager casts a spell on my half kilo of gorgeous
banknotes (Sultan Mehmet Fatih in purple, Mimar Sinan in
green), smiling modestly as he turns them into a few
wrinkled fifty dollar bills. Folded in a sheet of carbon paper
(Dr Norbert says the Post Office x-ray machine can't see
through it) and slipped inside a birthday card (another of
Norbert's tips), I lick the flap and kiss it goodbye.

But first my walk through the city. Even in the back
streets in the winter dark, with my money bulging like a
brick in my pocket, I never felt uneasy. The bars and grilles
on every ground floor window show that Turkey has
thieves too, but the policeman I saw on my first walk
leading a man by the ear down to the station suggested
traditional black and white theft. When two young Turks
dressed as punks appeared one day on the Galata Bridge, I
didn't know whom to sympathise with: them, so self-

conscious in their chains and daubed leather jackets, or the hurt, bewildered-looking crowd who stared at them.

The Galata Bridge crosses the Golden Horn, the spur of water cutting in from the Bosphorous. I often think, looking down at its oily green skin, that the name should have been given to the old city, the rhino horn of land pushing from Theodosius's wall out to the Seraglio Point, gold when the sun is on the rooftiles. Walking these small hills, supposedly seven in memory of Mother Rome, it is impossible to get lost. Lost for a while in a deep street, you get your bearings as you climb again and see some landmark: the ochre buttresses and flat mushroom dome of St Sophia, the arches of Valens's aquaduct, or the carbolic redbrick reformatory which turned out to be the old Greek *lycée* of Fener.

Again, all the old churches face east, sure as arrows; all the mosques, of course, face south-east, so you are never short of a compass. Surely the mid-nineteenth century, when Christians forgot to or no longer thought it important to orient their churches, is a useful benchmark from which we can trace the end of traditional religion in the West? With that break from the past, we leave the idea of a church as something natural to the earth, bound to it, springing from it, moving with the earth always into the eternally rising sun. It happened, I suppose, at the same time people stopped orienting their houses, when the rules tacit and immemorial for the direction the poorest cottage opened to fell away; in short, when Europe began its move from a country to a city civilisation.

When I visited here first, in the early sixties, it was the cripples I noticed, and the dark: half and quarter human shapes paddling in rubber basins through the flare of tilley lamps; all, nearly, gone in a generation. Now it is the prostitutes I notice, picking their way through bright lit mud along rush hour Vatan Caddesi. The traffic jams, a car door opens, a girl darts like a minnow, the car door shuts and the traffic stutters on another fifty yards. It's crude compared with Cumhuriyet Caddesi. I was up there, passing the Hilton with Ceyun, one of the Turkish teachers, the other evening when a Mercedes cruised alongside a tall, olive-legged young woman. I remarked that she was the most handsome I had seen since I came to Istanbul. "She's a man," Ceyun said, and as if to prove his point he pointed to another long-legged model. I stared, but could not see through the skin of flawless femininity.

Down on Vatan Caddesi the traffic jams are caused by the new Metro excavations, winding like an exposed giant intestine along one side of the boulevard-motorway. (In each huge section of concrete drain-pipe, a man lay sleeping.) The cutting grazes past Fenari Isa Cami, the Jesus Mosque, where someone has bridged it with a plank, and I crossed. Once the Church of Constantine Lips, a forgotten Byzantine nobleman with a memorable name, the mosque reveals the ease of its transition, in fact suggests a fundamental likeness of mind: the old church narthex turning naturally into the vestibule where shoes are left off; a niche in the old apse becoming the *mihrab* facing Mecca.

Indeed down in Istanbul's oldest church, St John Baptist of Studius, the (now ruined) Imrahor Cami, the Moslems had no need to build a courtyard with a place to wash feet, for there the church narthex was preceded by an atrium. Where did the early Christians take that tradition from? The synagogue? The temple? Their feet washed, the Christians no doubt left their shoes in the narthex as the Moslems do now. I spent a lot of time all winter last thinking of washed feet as I walked stilt-high with slabs of mud growing under my shoes. Even today, inside the Isa Cami, I could hear quarter tons of it dropping from JCB scoops into the lorries along the Metro trench; and always, everywhere in Istanbul, the ricochet of the piledriver at work on the new Galata Bridge, hammering into the bedrock below the mud. That is the best compass of all. In spring when the smog came down with the rain and my glasses were smeared black, all I had to do was follow that PA! pa-pa PA! which makes the city shake.

Constantine Lips, St Theodore's, Pammarakaristos, St Irene's – Edmund passes on the names like racing tips – these old Byzantine church mosques are the poor relations now, outstripped by the great Sultans' foundations of the sixteenth, seventeenth, eighteenth centuries – Suleymaniye, Beyazit, Sultan Ahmed, Fatih. Some, St Saviour's in Chora, not only survive but improve, their mosaics and painting restored, admission fees charged: museums. But the others are sad, empty places, smelling of damp; green streaks spreading over the whitewash that covered the Christian paintings, and pigeons flying through the broken bottle-end windows.

Yet in these places, where a pagan temple column did service in a Christian church, and the marble tail of a Christian peacock is woven into the lattice of a minaret balcony, or where at the flick of a rug a mosaic below comes to life, you can feel your way back to that shadowy Byzantine world where the emperor was still divine; where every winter solstice his Christian majesty mimed the reappearance of the sun which he personified. For he was the earthly image of the sun, was depicted with the nimbus as the Roman emperor had been, and the saints would be, alongside his empress in the holiest places within the church. But the Byzantines could not have depicted, say, Justinian and his wife, the whore Theodora, in St Sophia unless their divine status dwarfed their human one. These people saw the Pope in Rome as their pagan forebears saw him – as a fanatic threatening the unity of civilisation.

Take Claudianus. In town last week with Tom (at last the sun has driven him out of his yellow hiking boots – he bought instead a pair of sky blue espadrilles), I bought an odd volume of the Greek Anthology. Claudianus (AD 370-410) is represented by two epigrams which suggest what the Byzantine world must have been like:

"Newly revealed, Lord of the sky, born of old time, new-born Son, ever existing and pre-existing, highest and last, Christ, coeval with Thy immortal Father, in all ways like Him."

And, the pagan breaking through:

"Have mercy on me, dear Phoebus; for thou, drawer of the swift bow, wast wounded by the swift arrows of Love."

What was that paganism? I wondered as I went down the hill through the clotted streets. (A girl in an "I've been to Carnaby Street" T-shirt bleeding a pullet into the dust; a woman in a car tyre armchair spinning wool from a brown fleece – the naked sheep foraging nearby in a heap of empty tins.) Extremes of emotion – pride, cruelty, awe – struck from man's first encounter with the world about him? Christianity had been the leaven in the lump; but what when the bread was eaten? Gobbled up by – what? Science? Cities? Religion? What was left then?

"Christ is life", "Christ is Joy", "You are the Church", the young priests and nuns say as they run like hares into social work, apply for transfers to South America, flee convents and monasteries for housing estates, factories; anything, anywhere to escape the emptiness they sense in the old husk.

In the sun, the dust blowing down the streets hid the loose cobblestones. It was hard to think, too, dodging the stove pipes jutting head-high from the rotting old black timber tenements. There was no need to think (I thought ...), when down the last hill I stood into Nuruosmaniye Cami to take the shade and cool off before seeing the bank manager: the huge mosque was empty as usual and dark except for the ring of lamps suspended from the dome, hanging six feet above the carpet; then from beyond the light I heard a single voice, a woman's, at prayer, gasping out as if parching and calling for water the single word, "Allah", over and over – "Al-lah! ... Al-lah!" – a sound in the silence as deafening as the noise of rain beating down.

2 May 1988

Riots at yesterday's May Day march in Taksim. The *Daily News* reports, "Two persons" shot dead by police.

5 May 1988

I asked Tom did he think he'd be here next year?

Tom: "I'll have to drink about that."

7 May 1988

Istanbul sounds.

The muezzin, of course: "ALLAH AK-BAR ...!" five times a day from a thousand loudspeakers, rising and falling, scattering, uniting, like a flock of pigeons.

The milkman: "*SÜT! Süt-süt-süt ...!*" The tendons in his throat stretched stiff as skewers.

The vegetable lorries crawling like carnival floats down the streets all day; the boy in the back standing knee-deep in baskets, barrels, bags, basins, singing into his microphone: "*Tamates ... patates ... zeytin ... karpuzzzz!*"

The balloon man – with a hundred of them sometimes floating in a cloud, the strings tangled about his arm; rising on tiptoe sometimes as if he might take off: "*Balon!*"

Mothers' voices from the balconies in the evening, calling up their children: "Umut! Esra!" Later – a lost child calling its mother, "*Anné!*"

And at night, the lonely sound of the policeman's

whistle, fading into silence, then answered by another faint whistle from the next street: "Fioeee ... "

8 May 1988

Dr Norbert asked a few of us out to dinner last night. He likes organising these little treats. We went to the *Reshat Marmara*, a nightclub restaurant down by the sea. Lots of glamorous single women moving about. It took me about an hour to realise they were tarts. When I mentioned it to Tom, he shook his head and looked at me in wonder: "For someone who's knocked about, you're very innocent."

Norbert was in reflective mood, reminiscing about former days in Africa. Over the roast quail, he talked of his pastoral work in Soweto: "Hard work, hard uphill work and yet, looking back, they were my happiest days ... " In Nigeria, queuing outside a bank one day, an army officer tried to slip in front of him; Norbert "put him in his place. That got me fourteen days in 'the cooler'."

"What was that like?" We were like children listening to a parent in rare, communicative humour.

"Please ... *please!*" He closed eyes, pressed fingertips to the hazel toupee. "And yet I miss old 'Lagos on Sea'."

"You never think of going back there?"

"Too late now, I'm 'out of the game' now. Fifty-five. 'All the fives,' as they say."

"I'm nearly all the fours myself."

"Not enough, not enough, Adrian, to soothe the pain. Geoffrey, come and sit beside me, let me feel younger than you!"

When we got back to the wardrobe, he found he had left his keys in his flat, locked himself out. Together we went down the corridor, all standing about the door, fiddling with the handle. "Oh shit," he said eventually and quite suddenly lifted a foot, kicking with the heel of his shoe against the door. If I hadn't seen it, I wouldn't have believed he could do it. The door – less the lock and a jagged piece of wood broken off with it – flew open.

Spotlessly bare inside, except for that black high-crowned hat on the counter.

12 May 1988

A couple on the ferry boat. The girl, about twenty-two: soft dark colour, black oily rich hair, short, tied up at the back in a small ponytail with a white rubber band; goldy neck, the creases dark lines; blue check shirt, the collar showing over a light blue crew-neck jersey; a woollen plaid skirt; fine but strong legs; old black boots; a shoulder bag of Turkey carpet stuff. In Dublin, complexion changed, she would be a university student *à la mode*. This girl was as far from that as the head from the tail of a penny. The boy, about the same age: her brother or her husband? Clear high forehead, old clothes – jeans and poor shoes; a thin moustache; stroking his mouth as he spoke. They kept smiling slightly, as if they were brother and sister. She was beautiful; he was too. They weren't educated, I'd say. They had a full, simple expression – capable and balanced.

I was so absorbed in looking at them, I didn't notice the young man beside me until he touched my arm. It was the red-nosed student I had met last autumn in the tourist bar. Much redder now, with gin flowers spreading out over his face. He asked me for a drink. I lied, said I had promised to meet someone. He looked as if he was going to cry again, but smiled as he said in his perfect English: "A promise is a promise."

16 May 1988

The unfamiliar makes the familiar seem doubly strange.

Furze bushes, ash trees, granite ... but eagles circling overhead, wild bear crashing high up in the woods. The trees grow up the mountains on either side, roots bursting out of the slope, wrapping around boulders and burrowing down into the earth again; up and up for a thousand metres.

Evening, and the sounds carry. A man shouting "Allahallah!" in a "Christ give me patience" voice; then the crack of a stick and a dog's howl. Ten minutes later the dog appears, followed by an ass laden with firewood picking its way down the track, followed by the man. Smiles, presses hand to heart, passes on. Below on my left the river goes down in loud falls. Up in the woods – another sudden crackle of twigs. I didn't care. I had such a terrible hangover I just wanted to go on walking, breathing in the air.

I bought this exercise book in Thermal, a spa high above the eastern shore of Marmara where I slunk this morning; spent an hour in the *hamam*, a Byzantine-looking place with dish-cover-sized cupolas; maybe even older, judging by fragments of marble relief (Herakles with his club, funeral banquets) cemented into the wall; lay on the marble in the bath room chatting with an Iranian doctor desperate for advice about getting a visa to England; sat in the steam room until the heat made me panic, then in the cold plunge; and then that long walk. But still I have this ringing hangover.

In the end, Dr Norbert got everyone an invitation to the famous British Consulate reception. "Handing them out like fish and chips," Geoffrey said in disgust. He carried his own card as reverently as a communicant the host. Looking at him in his toffee suede brogues and worsted suit, Edmund in his National Health glasses, Tom in his shining navy blazer, it struck me that this place is a bit like a museum, everyone unchanged since they left home. Although Tom's blue espadrilles, I admit, count as change.

"Go with the blazer, don't they?" – as we walked down to the taxi rank.

"British Consulate, please," Geoffrey said, as you'd say "High Street, Kensington" to a London cabbie. He fidgeted and looked at his watch all the way through the Bosphorous tail-back. When we finally got to the old embassy gates, he almost ran in.

"How about a quick one?" Tom said and Stephanie smiled, so Edmund and I went with them down the hill to the Pera Palace Hotel. Like most famous institutions, the Pera Palace is self-conscious, the doorman more like an actor. Even the guests have the unconvincing naturalness you see in film extras. It must be one of the last hotels in Europe to have disposable linen towels in the lavatory; although the dirt in Edmund's hands is so ingrained that when he had dried them, the towel was spotless.

"I could do with a shave," – as he looked at his white-stubbled face in the brilliantly lighted mirror.

"As the man says – " Tom scrubbing his hands on another yard of starched linen, dropping it into a brass-mouthed mahogany box, " – Shave it for tomorrow."*

A liveried attendant motionless as a caryatid against the wall.

When we got downstairs, Stephanie had ordered our drinks. She's a slender, tender young girl with heavy brown long hair and clear sallow skin – Pre-Raphaelite, according to Edmund. ("Do you *know* Rossetti's *The Merciless Lady?*") She wears gold granny glasses which make her look sexy, especially when she sees Tom and they light up. Tom gazed up at the marble arches of the Victorian Byzantine lounge for a moment and then, in impeccable Irish form, he turned his back on Stephanie and began a long

---

* His own remarks are better: over a large Çin-tonik at the theatre the other night – "No play is as good as the interval."

conversation with Edmund and me about his "ancestors".
The word came so naturally that I believed him. Anyhow,
over three Turkish Konyaks he traced his family back to a
great-great grandmother who had written verse admired by
Sir Walter Scott. After a fourth glass, he was quoting her:
couplets so banal they were hard to remember. Something
like this –

And now the mighty orb from high
Rolls down the rosy western sky
About he throws his parting fires
And in a blaze of gold retires
On every side we cast our eyes
Behold! the falling landscape dies ...

"Mmm." Edmund nodded thoughtfully. "Sounds English to
me."
"I've no English blood – " Tom standing up, swaying,
" – except on my knuckles."
Stephanie linked his arm and we went up the hill to the
Consulate gates, showed our invitations, were frisked by a
metal detector, and trod up Her Majesty's gravel, Tom
taking great pleasure from the run-down state the place was
in – "They were in the saddle long enough." etc. Upper
windows shuttered, distemper flaking, it could have been a
shabby English country mansion; but, then, the embassy
proper is in Ankara now.
In my aunt's home in Mayo there was a novel by Harold
Nicolson, *Sweet Waters*, set in this old embassy. Going into
it now brought back a memory – not of the novel,
completely forgotten, but of the book itself, its covers bright
with yellow mildew flowers; and even more clearly – I
expect writing about childhood these past months has
brought it to the surface – going into the parlour one
summer holiday afternoon, taking the wings off bluebottles

buzzing in the window, feeding them to spiders' webs in the sashes, and then lying stomach down on the worm-eaten couch to read that story set in Constantinople.

But no novel is so inventive as what happens. Now there is a mosque in Ballyhaunis, oriented through my aunt's bog towards Mecca. Now I was in the old embassy in Constantinople. Then, walking up the wide, red-carpeted staircase, the first person I saw was someone I knew from school.

Her Britannic Majesty's Consul was killing a flock of birds with one stone. The EFL teachers, the textbook trade, the audio-visual reps, the whole works of the English language machine were there; the English engineers too and their wives, talking about the new Bosphorous bridge as if it was a baby; and the Ex-Pat Pats, as Tom called them, boasting in a corner ("My brother-in-law's nephew is Colm Tóibín ... "). But Hugh, what on earth was Hugh doing here?

"Adrian ... !"

The voice, Hugh's hand pumping mine up and down, started the old school memory machine, flashing another picture back from thirty years: me taking a short cut across the croquet lawn, on my bike, turning numb as I saw Father Williams on the other side, even more numb as, instead of what I expected, he murmured simply, "Ah, not on the grass, Adrian ... "

" ... What on earth are you doing here?"

I had forgotten just how white a white shirt could be, how light the scent of eau de something could be and still be perceptible. Hugh still parted his hair schoolboy fashion, a third to the left, two-thirds to the right. I found myself addressing it, avoiding his eyes as I said, "Teaching." I introduced Tom, Edmund, Stephanie. "We're teaching English."

"So is Catharine!"

Handsome, arched-eyebrowed Catharine.

"Actually, her real job is restoring old porcelain, but – "

Tom stared. Edmund shook hands with her as gravely as a bishop, then locked his long fingers behind his back.

"How about you?" I put in.

"Law! I'm with an Anglo-American firm here."

"Really?" Tom managed to lift a Konyak from a passing tray. "International law, Hugh?"

"Yes! Exactly! I might as well be at home – but Catharine gets about. She's practically fluent in Turkish."

"Darling, you know I'm not!"

"Darling, you are!"

Catharine placed a Mmm-muh! kiss on Hugh's cheek.

"What's the company called?" Forehead glistening, Tom swayed forward to catch the reply.

"Wright and Casey."

"Ah yes – "

"Heard of us, have you?"

"Ah no – I just … "

"Actually, we do have *one* Turkish client – Mr Özal's government!"

Tom nodded, took out a crushed packet of Turkish cigarettes. "Smoke, Hugh?"

Oh Hugh, dear polite Hugh, smoking your only vice, politeness your refuge and your strength – be polite, I prayed, take the bloody cigarette. Hugh smiled, waved a finger right and left in refusal as he went on talking. "A nice guy, Özal, as a matter of fact. We had tea with him the other day – Catharine talks English with Mrs Özal and … "

Another waiter went by and Tom took another drink, and suddenly he was gone: eyes glassy, voice slurring. He stumbled up the stairs, Edmund and Stephanie following to take his arms.

" … they asked if we'd like to go *hunting!* Seemed amazed when we told him we didn't go in for that sort of thing!" Hugh shook his head in amazement. We talked of a story the newspapers were making a meal of – Mr Özal burying his mother next to the tomb of Suleyman the Magnificent, and then the conversation stopped as suddenly as the Bosphorous rush hour traffic.

"Isn't it *extra* – " Catharine looking up at the ceiling, " – *ordinary!*"

"The Ionian white and gold – as Neddy Burke used to say. How's he getting along?"

We jerked forward on old school news: Slush Morton … Dippy Farrell … then stopped finally like Ali's minibus.

"Look, why don't we meet for a drink some evening?" Hugh took a card from a wallet – "Darling, do you have a pen?" Catharine took a pen from a handbag, wrote a number on the back of the card, said "That's home," and handed it to me with the rather aggressive smile you get from professional men's secretaries when they're handing over the bill.

Upstairs in the reception hall Tom was propped against a doric column, another glass of Konyak in his hand – held out, moving from side to side as if it was a key he was trying to get into a lock. Dr Norbert, like a priest at a Confirmation, was hovering by HM Consul's elbow, introducing his teachers one by one. But Geoffrey wasn't going to be confirmed so simply. As the Consul shook his hand, Geoffrey somehow spun him around so they stood with their backs to us, Geoffrey murmuring some anecdote in his ear. One by one the rest of us drifted off, Stephanie and I wandering into the next room, then the next, big empty salons; waltzing a few steps to ghost music – she had had a few too; sitting down then on a couch underneath a portrait of King Edward VII – appropriately. (Who said a diary without an incriminating entry was a lie?) I made a pass at her, hopelessly sudden. So far as I remember, she handled it very well, standing up smiling, leading the way back to the reception hall where Geoffrey was still gripping the Consul by the elbow. With Stephanie at his side again, Tom perked up. Turning his back on her, he began talking to me –

"All the same, these dos. Drink and fuck all else. I was at the Paddy's Day bash in Rome once – ever at the Irish embassy there? Labels on everything. Sit on a chair and someone comes up to you, says, 'I'm afraid that's seventeenth century.' Labels on the backs of the bloody statues – for fear someone'd rip them off ... "

I avoided his glazed gaze – and across the hall saw Hugh wave goodbye, a fingertip flutter. I got a drink for myself, then another, another. Nothing so sad as reminders that the past is so utterly past.

18 May 1988

Istanbul smells:
Petrol fumes. Fresh bread, cloth, leather. Water on hot cobblestones. Parched grass. Sea air. Sun-hot car metal. Burning fat, charcoal. Drains. Lemon Cologne.

19 May 1988

In the past year inflation has almost halved the value of my pay. To make it up, I have been giving English lessons to Selma, my bank manager's daughter.

"*Doomed* to be good at one thing," Edmund said when I pointed her out. Selma is a sixteen-year-old beauty who thinks of boys all day long. Every Saturday evening her father collects me in his car, bringing Selma along so she can talk English to me on the way back to their house. He wants value for money.

"Selma, *konush*!" (talk) he snaps as Selma looks out the car window at the boys. Luckily, Mr Seyid has no English and he nods in contentment as Selma comments in English on everything going by in trousers.

"He's too small ... He's too old ... He's too fat – but he looks rich."

"What about them?" I pointed out some handsome young building workers one evening, amusing themselves throwing a knife, sticking it into a heap of sand.

"They're too stupid."

"How do you know?"

"They must be – to become workers like that."

"*Tamam*, Selma." Her father nodded, pressing his fingers about his thumb in appreciation of this long sentence. He turned to me – "Selma, *nasil?*" (How is she?)

"*Güzel kiz,*" I said. (A beautiful girl.)

Wrong answer, Adrian. Mr Seyid frowned and chucked back his head in disagreement. To have a beautiful daughter, he tells me, is not good. He wants Selma to be a doctor, a vet, a bank manager, an English teacher. Every week he promises her something new if she does well in the exams. This evening it's a video-recorder.

"Aie! Baba!" Selma kissed him on top of his head and said to me, "Then I can watch *Who's that Girl!* Madonna – she will be in Londra this summer?" Selma is going on the school trip to England.

At home, she runs to her room to change all her clothes. Noise of drawers slamming open and shut as if she's already packing her bags for England. Mr Seyid cries "Selma!" and looks at his watch. She shoots out in the corridor in a new blouse and knickers. "ALLAHALLAH!" he shouts and she disappears, reappearing thirty seconds later in a white miniskirt. Mr Seyid says something to her and then draws the door shut on us and retires to the kitchen, where he and his wife tiptoe about so they won't disturb us.

"What did he say, Selma?"

"He say if I learn English good, then I can be rich and buy beautiful things." Their sitting-room is full up with baroque junk furniture and a shocking oil painting of luminous white-maned horses drinking from a baby blue lake. Each time a mosquito appears, Selma jumps up onto the table and swats with her *Kernel English*, glancing down then into the street where the boys hover like moths about the lamp post.

One night the electricity failed. The light bulb had hardly darkened when Mr Seyid appeared with a candle, stood it on the table, then lay down on the couch behind us as chaperone. As the candle burned low and Mr Seyid fell asleep, I could understand what romance there must be in a Turkish courtship.

Sometimes, to relieve her boredom, Selma cries, "*Anné! Servis!*" (Mother! Service!) and her mother tiptoes in, a fat woman who might be thirty or sixty, and takes Selma's order for apple tea.

After the lesson, Selma vanishes to her room – more slamming of drawers – and Mr and Mrs Seyid appear, to ask me about her progress. He pours me a glass of Scotch, turns on the colour TV and then his mother slips in, a shrewd-faced, wrinkled old countrywoman with a white muslin head-dress. She draws it up over her eyes as Tina Turner struts and sings, peeping over the veil in fascination and exclaiming, "Aie!"

Not good enough for Mr Seyid. He turns down the sound and calls Selma. She returns reluctantly – in a new outfit – to translate his questions.

Poor Selma. Eight hours in school. Four hours' homework. An hour and a half private tuition. And now this.

"My father, he says – are you … ?" She yawns, blesses herself.

"A Christian? Yes."

"*Evet, Baba.*"

"Selma! *Ingiliz!*"

"Yes, Baba, he is a Christian."

"*Tamam* ... " Mr Seyid nods, taps fingernails on the red-varnished tabletop as he thinks up more conversation, smiling again as Selma says to me, "Madonna – she wears a ... '*haç*'?" She outspreads her arms.

"A crucifix?"

"Yes! Aie! I *love* Madonna!"

20 May 1988

A funeral at the corner mosque today: small crowd – a dozen poorly dressed old men against the wall chatting and shaking hands and watching another dozen expensively dressed people in the courtyard. The coffin, covered with a green chenille rug, was put on the back of a Camion pick-up truck painted the same Islamic green. The Imam appeared with a big Koran under his arm, tucked up his gown skirts, ducked into the passenger seat (knocking his turban sideways) and they drove away.

The legless lottery ticket-seller who sits at the corner in his bicycle-wheel wheelchair said – he likes to practise his English on me – that it was the old army officer who had died, the poker straight man I used to meet at the bus stop, the one who read Poe's *Tales of Mystery and Imagination*.

21 May 1988

Geoffrey giving me yesterday's *Financial Times*: "Couldn't get it for love or money in Saudi. Here I am in some potty little Turkish shop – and I just pick it up!" He buys it to follow some old shares he owns in something. He dreams of making a killing and retiring to England ("I'd be off like a bunny."). This evening he directed my attention to a story

116

about Sir James Goldsmith winning a libel action, sighing enviously: "Yes, he took 'em hat, arse and coat-tails." He tells me how once in Saudi, hearing that the price of gold was going up, he ran across Riyadh in one hundred and twenty degrees of heat and bought all the gold he could – £600 worth. The price went down. He sold and bought £300 of platinum instead.

All the time his radio is playing, a fruity BBC voice evoking the beauties of the English countryside: " ... Silence too on the upland moors, save for the plaintive 'Bek-bek-bek' of a grouse amongst the heather, ling and bell, their purple splendour muted now ... "

He's bought one of those blue glass eyes people here have everywhere to ward off the Evil Eye. Showing it to me – he's glued it on his apartment door – he went on to tell me, without a grain of irony, that his wife is coming out next week.

22 May 1988

Bayram. For the last month I have been woken at four every morning by the thunder of a drum going by below my window, warning all Moslems that dawn is coming, that if they are to have breakfast before the fast begins, they must get up now. Some of the school children followed Ramazan strictly and in class sometimes there were thumps as a boy or girl fainted and a head dropped onto the desk top. The school is strictly secular and lunch was served as usual at noon every day, when those children took pride in walking about the playground, abstaining.

Ramazan seems quite different from Christian Lent. There is not, that I can see, any suggestion of penance; more an assertion of strength, a flexing of the muscles of self-control. Looking at the Anatolian building workers on the sites spit out saliva rather than swallow it and ease their burning throats, I was reminded of the men I see in the *hamam* chop-chopping the sides of their hands on each other's backs, scrubbing each other with rough towels, walking up and down each other's spines, sometimes until they scream; suffering in the steam room and the ice cold plunge. Walking out afterwards, they have the same proud poised air the building workers can have each evening at sunset. There is no signal gun fired here. Our unofficial announcement was the *Lara* song from *Dr Zhivago* played by an ice cream van that shot into action as the top rim of the sun slid out of sight.

"That's Ramazan for you," Tom remarks. "Easter every evening."

"*Oruc bitti*," the Turkish saying goes – "My fast is ended." One of the senior school boys said it with real feeling yesterday, when Deirdre appeared without a bra.

Inci: "Aie! Dede! I can see your ... buttons!"

(Deirdre tells me she has a new Turkish lover, Halil. If I had anything to exchange for these confidences, I would give it gladly. But what can compare with Deirdre's stories? One night at the height of love-making, Halil cried out, "I'm going!" Deirdre sat up and Halil cried, "Pardon! Pardon! I'm ... *coming*!".)

The Bayram is a school holiday too and for the remaining few days of it I decided to take a break (novel almost complete). Inci was going over to her family home in Thrace and I took a lift with her. From there, I had decided to take a bus down the coast, cross the Dardanelles and make a full circle back up to Istanbul.

Suddenly it's summer. The storks have drifted back. One night the cicadas started, throbbing like the day's heat from cracked walls and paths. A municipal lorry went through our estate, a cannon behind firing smoke until only the tenth-floor flats showed above the clouds, but still the mosquitoes hatched out. Already the sun was invisible in a white-blue sky as we drove across the Bosphorous bridge, and soon we were on the flat straight road to Greece we had taken last autumn. Tower blocks webbed with scaffolding then were finished now, new homes, beehive full, and the scaffolding – those random-looking rough-cut poles – were on new tower blocks another kilometre out into the country. You get a glimpse between them sometimes, like a view between trees of the sea: rooftiles shimmering to the horizon.

We came to a roadblock, a car parked crossways, a body of armed police. (Twelve more of the escaped prisoners, the biggest haul yet, were caught recently in Edirne as they tried to cross into Greece.) Our car was searched, waved on by submachine gun snouts and we were out in the rich land of Thrace; windows rolled full down, but not a breath of cool air in the breeze; overtaking tractor trailers full of women on their way to another day's work in the fields. On either side, the telegraph wires were strung with bee-eater birds, petrol blue breasts glittering against the sunlight.

Looking at the fields going by and the people in them, I thought of what that Dutch boy Frederic had said about Turkish painting at our indoor picnic party last spring. Looking at Turkish modern art in the style of Western painters makes you realise how local, very local, the latter are. Turkish landscape and people done – say – in a highly focused, passionate Van Gogh style, seem silly, meaningless and over-refined. For, I thought – maybe in just some other refined way – the people we passed really *were* in the fields, in a way unfamiliar to Western Europe now, a way hard to describe, being more an attitude of mind than of body.

The old men sitting sideways, legs tucked down in the drills as they weeded the ridges; the girls' flowery head-dresses moving just above the green maize heads, old women sitting in circles, cross-legged in their flowery pyjama trousers, binding onions and carrots into bunches; even the young men, the few, in tractors seemed part of the place, whirling up prongs and blades that flashed blue bright as the bee-eater birds darting from the wires. They were anonymous, yet all had still some of that certainty any majority has. Any day now they will be a minority; a generation ago three-quarters of the Turkish population were on the land; now it is exactly half.

Like most of the Turkish teachers in our school, Inci seems to be well-off. Her mother lives in a small, expensive apartment overlooking Marmara. Pale waxed parquet floors spread with comfortable old rugs; a framed, tinted photo of a tough-looking man in army uniform; prayer beads and an open Koran on a wine table by a window seat. If travel broadens the mind, it is only by showing how same the world is everywhere. Inci moved about her home with the unease of any young woman trying to keep her mother at arm's length; moving constantly even while she talked, glancing at a newspaper as she answered a question, scratching her back on a glass-fronted china cabinet while her mother talked; drifting off into the kitchen, returning with tea and pastries. It was the sort of conversation I once thought belonged only to Ireland and Irish weather: grey cloudy silences, conversation breaking out like the sun, sinking back again. It seemed shocking in such brilliant blue-skied weather. Inci ended it abruptly – when her two sons suggested a swim – kissing her mother's hand in Bayram greeting and pressing it to her forehead.

I had some hours to wait before my bus came, so I went with them. Once in the car, Inci's wistful face cleared; speaking English again, she pointed out the sights. A small mosque by Sinan. Two guards with rifles, smoking on a parapet: the jail. A big jail for a small town, I remarked and Inci's younger son said, "We have many *çingene*, pardon – gypsies." A serious boy, he wants to be a soldier and talked with gloomy fluency about the great days of the Ottoman empire – "*Misir* (Egypt) ... *Fas* (Morocco) ... *Cezayir* (Algeria) ... all gone. It is terrible."

The elder boy, absorbed by his Walkman music and a scuff on his white Nike boots, spoke only to point out family possessions: a tower block rising from a field here, another there. We touched eighty on the highway out of town, slowed and turned down a track to the sea, stopping at a cottage by the shore.

It too belonged to Inci's family. It was her father's home, she explained as we changed on the veranda – doubly shaded by a vine grown wild. From behind the shuttered windows came the rustling of mice, stopping each time she spoke. " – But he left to fight with Ataturk and after he never come back."

"He was killed?"

"Not in the war. After the war he worked, he work too much – "

("Very much, *Anné*," – both sons corrected her.)

"Pardon! After the war all the peasants work very much. They wanted to make a new country. Ataturk say this. My father worked until he can buy a *parcelle* of land from old *Yunan* – pardon, Greek – family. In this part all the rich people were Greek ... "

Her father worked and worked, bought more and more land. Then one morning he was driving to the market to sell melons. He was so tired that he stopped his horse and lay down to sleep in the cart. It was still dark. A lorry coming from the same direction crashed into the cart and – Inci clapped hands together – "It break him like a melon."

("Broke," said the two boys as one, and Inci said again,

"Pardon! Pardon! Always I confuse present tense with past perfect.")

After the first small shock, the water was warm, the seaweed flowers – white and red crimp-leaved carnation shapes – clear six feet below; salty water pressing upwards, making floating natural. Inci floated alongside, still pointing out sights. A speck far across the bay prompted this story:

"A king once lived over there with his only, beautiful daughter. All the young men want to marry her, but the king say – No, the only man who will have her is the man who drive across the sea and take her. All the men come – " Inci pointed to the bracken and heather, deafening with cicadas, burning with heat, running down to the shore, " – and try to drive their horses and cars across the sea, but they fail. Then one man made this way – " she rolled over onto her stomach and, floating face down, pointed out, incredibly, a ramp of sea-smoothed stones just showing above the sand, going straight out to sea, " – and he drive to her, and he get her!"

The bay, shimmering in the heat like a fresh-forged horseshoe.

25 May 1988

The doors of St Sophia are of bronze and wood, decorated with a depiction of ancient simple doors. Every age looks back to a "simpler" age. Passing today, I went in and wandered about the acre of worn marble floor, looking at carved graffiti a thousand years old which still seem spray-gun new. A temple, then a synagogue, a cathedral and then a mosque and now a museum. The pillars like almighty tree trunks, the dome like the sky, remaining specks of mosaic sparkling like stars. Leaning against one of the columns, hands in trouser pockets, gaping upwards, mouth hanging half open – Edmund. He looked so unutterably lonely that I stole away out the doors again.

26 May 1988

Coming in this evening, going up the stairs, I heard a familiar cockatoo shrill: Séamus!

Sunburnt, more relaxed, he actually talked with me when I joined the others gathered about him. He's been in Israel for the past six months, working on a kibbutz, a farm growing vegetables. "Good moory soil." I hadn't known his father was a farmer.

He returned last week, went to Dr Norbert, who gave him "a smashing reference" and sent him off to a rival school whose headmaster employed Séamus on the spot.

27 May 1988

Sometimes going up in the lift we get out on the wrong floor, walk down the same-looking corridor and try our key in a door corresponding to our own. In this hot weather the doors are usually open. I was reading by the window this evening when Gail walked in undoing her blouse buttons, saw her mistake – no welcoming cat? – and strolled out again, all without even noticing me.

28 May 1988

Yesterday was Dr Norbert's birthday. He threw a party last night. Where to begin?

Lodos, they called the wind that beat up from the south-west all winter. Now it is the *Meltem*, the cooling summer breeze – carrying the stink of sewage. We sailed further down into Marmara, the air and water cleared; the ship's wake was silver with phosphorescence as dusk came down, the wind like honey. Everyone went to the party, our last treat before the June examinations. Irene appeared for the first time in public with Murat Bey, her arm in his, walking the deck in her croaking stiff, knife-crease blue jeans. Still the mahogany tights underneath, and the *Irish Independent* under her free arm; but there is something different about her, lovely as the *Meltem*. Tom was alone. Geoffrey and his wife sat apart.

"What a battle-axe," Edmund said. "She really wiped the *floor* with me."

Is a spouse like a mirror reflecting the other half? Seeing Geoffrey with his wife this past week has been like seeing him for the first time. As soon as she arrived, his visits to my flat stopped and in the street now he walks by without a word. One evening he did drop in for five minutes; I asked if he would take a cup of coffee, but he fidgeted and hurried back downstairs. The other evening my corkscrew was mislaid and I went down to borrow his. Shuffling his country gentleman long legs, he made small-talk on the threshold, until his wife called out, "Who is it?" and he called back, "I'm just talking to this Irish peasant!" and laughing, flustered, brought me inside.

Six feet tall, in high-waisted trousers that might have been cut for Geoffrey – if they weren't of pink crimplene – Judith is the boss. She poured me a stiff gin and tonic and sat me down to talk to, turning now and then as Geoffrey tried to open my bottle of wine. "Not that way! My God, it's not that long since you used one!"

Rattled, Geoffrey yanked at the cork and half of it broke off.

"What a bloody incompetent … " She turned back to me, topping up my glass and talking to me again. An interesting thing, upper class talk: swear words, vulgar words ("arseholes"), blanket words like "silly", "boring", "dim", and baby-talk words like "piggy" are all used to put down anything which might have to be taken seriously.

(I suppose it has its uses: we had a small earthquake last Tuesday night and as we all stood outside in the dark amongst the tower blocks, Judith's blasé booming "Ours is the wobbliest," calmed down Edmund, who was terrified.) Dr Norbert is "a dwarf". This approach keeps everything at arm's length where it can be laughed at, dismissed or confidently discussed. When Geoffrey drove the rest of the cork down into the bottle and showered his face with my wine, she said, "I thought you were staying off the stuff?"

But what a strange thing marriage is. There's a spring in his suede shoes now. Arm in arm with Judith, he walked the deck as happy-looking as Murat with Irene.

The Black Sea, fed by rivers pouring off the Russian plains, is cold and rushes down the Bosphorous through Marmara to the Aegean, whose briny warm waters are dragged north as an undercurrent. A half-decker went bouncing across this conflict, carrying a cow out to one of the islands, two men leaning on her back as casually as if she was a farm gate, smoking and chatting. Murat Bey joined us at the rails and intoned a Turkish proverb – "*Sen aga, ben aga, inekim saga?*"

"What's that?" Edmund enquired and, to our surprise, Irene translated at once – "You're a gentleman, I'm a gentleman, who's going to milk the cow?"

And seeing that Edmund is interested – Edmund is interested in *everything* – Murat recited another.

"*Ölümun ötesi kolay*" – "After death it's easy."

Murat has an enthusiasm for what he called "fuck lore". Edmund looked startled as a priest, running his long fingers through his silver mop of hair, until Murat went on to talk of "fuck dancing".

The dusky smudges enlarged, the white timber houses appeared and we got the scent of woodsmoke. *Büyükada* – The Big Island. The boat bumped against the pier and Dr Norbert appeared – "*Like* Prospero," as Edmund said. Irene led the way down the gangplank, stepping quickly away from a gold-toothed sailor who tried to help her. She ran a finger down the zip of her shoulder bag, linked Murat's arm again and laughed – "This is the life!"

"Any more on this boat?" Norbert scanned the crowd: working men in navy serge suits and flat caps, naval cadets in white, middle-class girls in jeans and trainers who might have been from Paris or New York but for their elaborate gold-clipped hairstyles. " ... No, just Turks." He makes the word sound disgusting. He led the way between the two machine-gun marines out into the village street.

"Well, Edmund!" Geoffrey squinting at his watch. "England should be just about declaring now."

"Eh?"

"At Lords. You know – the Test."

"I don't *follow* cricket."

No cars on the island, which adds to its unreality. Norbert walked along the rank of horse-drawn carriages, chose an ancient phaeton. There is something almost schoolboyishly perverse in the way at times like this Edmund automatically does the opposite: "I think I'll walk."

The jarvey cracked a six-foot plaited thong and the carriage rolled silently up the sandy village street between film-set perfect Ottoman houses. Uniformed maids. Boys on imported Raleigh bikes. A white-painted synagogue ... "*Yehudi* – " (Jews) the jarvey lapsed into his tourist guide patter, rubbing fingers on thumb " – *zengin* ... " (rich)

"Oh God." Dr Norbert stopped him with a yawn.

Cut off by the weather in winter, in summer the island is cut off by wealth. Even the horse droppings, caught on a sheet of blue cloth stretched between the shafts, their scent mingling with eucalyptus leaves crushed under hoof, suggested luxurious isolation.

"The only way to travel ... " Dr Norbert sighed as he lay back on the leather cushions, slipped into his sultan's posture: one leg flopping across the other, head lolling back, hand trailing over the carriage door in the warm night air. The fireflies were out, glowing and fading like Tom's cigarette.

"Hear Séamus is back."

"Back from the Holy Land."

"Landed on his feet all right."

"What is life, Tom – " Norbert rested cheekbone on fingertip, "what is life, if one cannot help another? The longer I live, the more I realise – "

"Happy birthday," Tom cut him short.

"Fifty-six. 'Five six – pick up sticks,' as they say. Ahead lies 'Seven eight – lick the plate!' More immediately ahead – next year. Adrian, can I 'bank' on you?"

"Afraid not. I'm going home."

"Ah me … And, Tom? 'Et tu, Tom?'"

Tom muttered something about an interview coming up. Hand swinging from side to side, Norbert sighed. "Where will I be without you all … ?"

We are never allowed to pay for anything on these outings. A generous tipper too, Norbert held out a ten thousand lira note, lengthways, between his fingertips, turning on his heel as the jarvey gave thanks, leading the way up the steep green hill.

A string of party lights hung along the veranda rails – yellow, blue, green, red. His tiny swimming-pool had been emptied and in it now a fire blazed, roasting a lamb spitted on an iron rod. Barish the houseboy, a cruelly lame young man in his twenties with the deathly white face of an El Greco saint, dragged his leg after him towards Dr Norbert. Murmuring together, they disappeared into the house. I wandered around the garden gloomy, the relief at finishing my novel gone; in its place – like a captain who has brought his ship to port and seen the passengers ashore – just emptiness and the prospect of another voyage … and then another. Long lazy orange cracks of summer lightning appeared and disappeared between mumbles of remote thunder. Vega, the glowing tip of Orpheus's Lyre, was near zenith.

When I got back to the bungalow, the roast lamb was in the kitchen, the spit ends resting on the backs of two chairs, fat rattling down like raindrops onto a carpet of tinfoil below, sparkling blue in the electric light.

"Father Norbert celebrating *Mass.*" Edmund had arrived.

Geoffrey: "Keep it down, old boy."

One by one we filed up to this altar where Norbert presided with his servant boy, who swung the knife mechanically, baring blue ribs, catching pound pieces of blue fatty flesh in paper plates and murmuring, "*Afiyet Olsun.*"

"Or as we say in English – *Bon appetit!*" Norbert handed us each a knife and fork wrapped in a green paper napkin – which turned red as we went outside again to eat.

"Hell!" from Edmund as he slipped down the steep slope, almost into the swimming-pool fire. Geoffrey caught his head on an overhanging branch. We ate sitting down, heels dug into the grass. Already the shop-talk had begun, growing louder with the wine: talk of past jobs and future jobs, of advertisements seen in Tuesday's *Guardian* or *The Times Educational Supplement*. Even Geoffrey turned away from his wife to join in, quizzing Marion about Nigeria.

"Any trouble getting the cash out?"

"Sure that's why I'm here!"

"In Morocco," Edmund said, "I used to put it in a thermos flask of *hot* coffee, then I used to cross into Spain and buy pesetas ... "

"Yerra, Edmund! Where would you get a thermos flask of hot coffee in Nigeria?"

"Slip into Gib then, did you, Edmund? Buy sterling? Used to see them at that wheeze when I was there." Geoffrey threw back his fairy-light tinted glass of orange juice.

"When was this?"

"This is going back a bit. I mean, TEFL-wise it was hell. Franco and all that. You know – private soldiers begging for cigarettes in the street. And the officers, for all the scrambled egg on their hats, they hadn't too damn much either."

"Well," Tom put in. "Say what you like about Germany – "

"I jolly well shall." (Judith)

"Still, you don't have that problem there."

"Damn useful thing, the DM," Geoffrey agreed as he got to his feet.

"Where were you there, Tom?"

"Mainz."

"Sure, I was there!" Even Marion was smiling. "Who were you with? Berlitz?"

"The old firm." Tom had another Efes and he was off, talking about New Year's Eve and the fireworks over the Rhine and the old people calling *"Alle is gutte,"* shouting almost as the music started suddenly, and then the dancing began; Dr Norbert up first, doing a shimmy in his tiger-striped kaftan, leading a conga all around the minute garden (Tom with his arms about Marion's waist) and back to the swimming-pool's edge, where he danced solo to clapping hands, his own hands clenched fists punching at the sky, his no-hips bumping side to side, the cream slacks red in the leaping flame light, glossy toupee catching the yellow, red, blue, green of the party lights, upturned face white in the moonlight, shrilling along to the words of the song –

You rock in the tree tops all day long
Hoppin' and a boppin' and a singin' your song
Rockin' Robin – boop! boop! Rockin' Robin ...

A crackling blaze as Barish threw the lamb's carcass – ribcage picked bare – into the fire.

1 June 1988

Umut, one of the children at school, looks just like a pig –
terrible, considering they all shudder even at the word
("*Domuz*"). Flat, upturned nose showing round nostrils,
small eyes, a big pink face; even his hair is like bristle. He
tries to be popular by showing off and, when the others
laugh, Umut gets excited, threshing his arms about, talking
so quickly his mouth slobbers – and then they all jeer and
he collapses. His father, an electrician, was in school today
doing some wiring job and Umut introduced me to him: a
gentle, handsome face – Umut's features undistorted – with
a look of indescribable sadness. He smiled, shook hands,
then took up his pliers and went on with his work,
snipping and splicing.

3 June 1988

In the PTT today, queuing at the Poste Restante counter,
there was a German girl a few places before me. A young
Turk standing behind her stared at the white blond hair
then, as if in a trance, put out finger and thumb and took
the end of a lock, felt it, let it go again. She never noticed.

It cuts the other way too. This evening I brought along
an old *Irish Times* to the Seyids to try Selma out on unseen
translation. She fastened on a photo of a blond young man.
"*Kim?*" (Who?) – she pointed, finger touching the fair head.
"*Bir Dakka!*" (One moment) – raised her finger and read
the paragraph aloud in a reverent voice –

" ... 'Not in the least!' Mark McGrath laughs at the
notion, lapsing into nutty, gutty Dublin tones – 'Ya boy ya!'
He pours us each another glass of wine, a nice chewy
Châteauneuf, then calls the waiter in snappy colloquial
Paris-speak which wins an approving smile from that most

discerning of critics. McGrath is one of the new, international breed of Irish artists, equally at home in … "

Good old McGrath, the urbane provincial, still on the run from your fear of being ordinary. Well at last you've touched a human heart.

"Aie!" Selma put her hands over her face and moaned, "How will I ever understand?"

(Mrs Seyid, from the kitchen: "SELMA!")

4 June 1988

Edmund: "So I put on the tape as usual and sat at the back of the lab, and what with the kips *yesterday* I must have dropped off. When I woke up they were all as quiet as bloody mice, looking at the video. Then I saw what it was. Buggers must have *switched* tapes. This bird stripped to the waist. Something called 'Love and Death in LA.' One girl was hiding her face in her hands from it. Still, it was in English … "

7 June 1988

Dr Norbert's gone.

To my surprise, I'm not a bit surprised. The rumours broke out everywhere this morning, like the news of the prisoners' escape from Metris last March.

Irene: "I hear he's in London."

Our school headmaster (his face as impassive as the badge of Ataturk's face in his lapel): "Yes, Dr Hopkins is not well."

Someone rang his secretary: "Dr Norbert had a heart attack on the plane to England. He was taken off at Rome and is in hospital in the Vatican. He is doing well."

By evening the rumours had settled down to a single version. The sixty-five children going to England this summer on the school trip had each paid £600 into a bank account. Norbert was given charge of it and flew to London to lodge it in a bank there. Instead, he transferred it to his own account and fled to Rome.

Irene, tapping out the sum on her pocket calculator: "I knew there was something wrong when he wasn't in *The Catholic Directory* ... Thirty-nine thousand pounds. *Sterling.*"

15 June 1988

A sudden, awful attack of homesickness.

What have I been doing this past week?
    Wandering about the city.
1. In the Sahaflar Çarsisi, the old book market in Beyazit: a cat curled up asleep, moving as the sun left him and standing-arching-yawning up from a copy of Casanova's *Memoires*, lying down again a few inches away in the warmth, curling up on a book entitled *The Demon of Dyspepsia*.

An old *hodja* blowing his nose between finger and thumb, shaking off the mucus once, twice; his rheumatic hand giving up then, he walked away trailing a gossamer thread sparkling in the sunlight.

2. Ran into Salih, on his way home from work, and we had a drink together – under the Galata Bridge; on the cheap, upstream side looking out on the new bridge which advances day by day from either shore. Suddenly, in comparison, the old bridge seems decrepit. You notice now, through broken planks patched with hardboard, the Golden Horn flowing below; hear the girders grinding against one another; notice the beer slanting in your glass as the whole structure sways. Flashing a lone 10,000 lira

note, Salih insisted on treating me to fried sheep's lung.

He earns 280,000 liras a month (about £100). Before this supermarket job, he worked in Izmir (250,000 liras plus free dormitory) for a Dutch firm making greenhouses.

"I hate them" – when I admired the mosque domes, grape blue in the dusk. He hates Turkey. Taking out a biro, looking round, he wrote IRA on the back of his hand, raised eyebrows, nodded, spat and rubbed the letters out again. He sees police spies everywhere. Wherever you go, he claims, one in ten will be an informer.

"*Ne Var?*" (What is it?) he snapped, as someone at the next table, hearing us speak English, leaned across to join in.

What does he usually do in the evening? By the time he gets home it is ten o'clock. His wife gives him dinner. Then – he ran his finger around the dial of his big jazzy wrist watch to 1am – "Drink raki, raki, raki … " This leaves him five hours sleep before he sets off to work again. Tomorrow, Friday, is his day off and the following Sunday, a rotating day off, falls to him – a conjunction seemingly as rare as an eclipse of the moon. "Ask the boss for Saturday too," I said, "and you'll have three days off."

"If I ask, he would cut out my – " he stuck out his tongue. "What is this in English?"

"Tongue."

"He would cut out my tongue." Taking out his biro again, he wrote the word in a notebook.

My head still reeling after a year of evenings at the typewriter (I still hear the keys hammering words), I hadn't the energy to speak Turkish; nor Salih. After his thirteen hours at the stall, he smells of vegetables: a celery-orange scent. The crowsfeet about his eyes stand out like the sinews on the backs of his hands. We sat across the table leaning towards each other, to make up for the silence.

Istanbul background sounds: click of finger-joints being

crackled, of worry beads, backgammon dice, cards, of samovar lids rising and falling with the steam; snatches of arabesque song lilted, whistled, hummed. Like an old engine turning over.

"*Hava güzel*," I said as we parted on the bridge. (Beautiful weather.)

"*Hava güzel*." Salih nodded. "*Türkiye güzel degil*." (Turkey isn't beautiful.)

When I looked back, he was still on the bridge, having his boots polished: black, high-heeled, silver-tipped winkle-pickers; one foot on the block, one hand on hip, chest out, ignoring the boy kneeling at his feet. A pasha.

3. Dinner with Edmund in the *Dört Mevsim* (Four Seasons) restaurant. As a young man, he told me, he used to go up into the Lancashire moors in the mist until he was lost, then see could he find his way home again. Sad smile: "I *always* could." Once in Morocco he was offered a baby for sale. "You could buy anything in Morocco."

Walking home, he suggested we go through the brothels. I had been there before, one Christmas morning years ago. Arriving in Istanbul from the East and walking about the streets, I was caught up in a crowd swirling about an alleymouth, carried down like a leaf and eddied in a narrow iron gateway ("*Kafes*" is the place's Turkish nickname, "The Cages") between two policemen with rubber truncheons – still there to frisk us.

The same smell: urine and roasting chestnuts. Two workmen were digging up a bit of the street, arguing about a broken sewage pipe. A half-dozen Italian sailors in snow white ducks. Two German businessmen with an after-dinner glaze to their lean grey faces. The same old men watching soccer on TV in a tea shop at the end of the cul de sac. Green and mauve distempered rooms.

A blind old man was sitting for some reason in one of

the lobbies chatting with the girls. One of them, smoking a cigarette, a paper flower in her hair, crept up behind him, took his cap and ran off with it, laughing. The blind man got up in sudden rage, waving his white stick, other hand outspread groping, as if playing Blind Man's Buff. She came behind him and gave him a shove and he fell over.

A woman aged about sixty, bare bottom wrinkled elephant grey, sliding slowly backwards down a bannister. A red-haired, freckled, Irish-looking girl whispering to a Chinese-looking girl dozing in her lap. A striking, dark brown-skinned girl, nipples and finger and toenails painted the same signal red, advanced on the crowd like a tiger. The young shaven-headed soldiers stepped back giggling nervously, pressed forwards again; jumped back as she lunged with a stroke of red fingernails. A blank, tense expression on all the men's faces; lips shut, breathing through nostrils. All men look the same in a brothel.

I was quite nervous about doing it, but suddenly decided to. I suppose all the wine I had drunk at dinner gave me courage. "Edmund," I said, "do you have a son?"

"No." Calmly abrupt, as he pressed the Ventolin to his mouth.

He pointed out his girl to me, Deniz: pasty-faced, with a pop star fringe, smoking a cigarette. She looked blankly past him. Edmund began to say something as we walked home, stopped, began again: "Do you know, she wanted to *mount* me!"

4. The government has begun an anti-smoking campaign. Everywhere the poster is appearing, showing a man smoking a cigarette, the smoke wreathing up into the shape of a dragon that writhes downwards, jaws open wide to devour him.

5. I met Tom wandering about the museum garden amongst

the rubble of the past: stele, sarcophagus, stone dolphin fountain mouths, marble wreaths, headless orators holding forth scrolls, headless warriors with lions' mask breastplates, capitals cut into fantastic flower displays.

Tom: "And I suppose some poor ballocks got eighteen pence a day for carving that stuff."

Heroic art was the ideal vision of those who did not have to endure poverty, executed by those who did.

Tom says that Séamus has a girlfriend, an English teacher in his new school.

Tom: "I asked him if he'd screwed her yet."

"Well?"

Tom, imitating the Galway shrill – "Everything but!"

A private soldier was sitting beside us and we chatted. His name was Mehmet; he had been in Berlin for the past few years living with his uncle, who owns a taxi there. A single blue button on his cap showed he was the lowest rank private. As soon as his eighteen months National Service is over, he will go back to Berlin, where he hopes to inherit the uncle's taxi. Our chat was ended by a single word – "*Asker!*" (Soldier).

An officer with, as Geoffrey would say, lots of scrambled egg on his hat, was coming out of the museum. About fifty; trousers creased sharp, worn slightly off his shoes which were slightly high-heeled. Hat tilted down, peak resting on the bridge of his nose. He walked in soft lounging little movements. His wife alongside: a dyed blonde in a fur coat; unhappy smart face. Mehmet loped to the car, a lacquer-bright black Mercedes with navy blue blinds in the back window, and drove the few dozen yards to the foot of the museum steps, sprang out, saluted, opened the back door for wife and officer, shut it on them, drove away.

Every other street in Istanbul has a military and police

outfitters, always with a few men looking in the window at the display of stripes, pips, crossed sabres, lanyards, gold braids.

Tom, as if embarrassed – looking away at the army Mercedes going down the museum avenue, told me he had been to his interview, got the job. It's at the University of Kadiköy, a glorified technical school in a few dilapidated concrete buildings, but still ... "A university man at last," I said, "like your father."

Tom: "Ah fuck off!" (Hesitant smile.)

6. Drinking-water queues at pumps, taps, municipal tankers; tin buckets, clay jugs, plastic drums; an old couple sitting a brimming basin into a go-car and pushing it home.

7. Latest Norbert rumours (they spring up daily, like fables about the early Christian martyrs): a) he was involved with the Mafia; they set his feet in cement and dropped him in the Bosphorous; b) he fled to a cottage he owns in Rooskey, County Leitrim; c) he died of a heart attack on the plane, was buried in Rome.

19 June 1988

In the evening I gave my last lesson to Selma before the exams. Mrs Seyid had dinner prepared for me: iced *Ayran* – a yoghurt drink; aubergine salad; *köfte* – spiced meatballs – with saffron rice; and *baklava* – a honey cake. When I had taken my coffee, she took the thimble cup, upturned it on the saucer and read the grounds for me. I am going to inherit a large sum of money; I am going on a long journey. I said the second was true: I was going home at the end of the month.

Afterwards, Mr Seyid hinted at how the first might also be fulfilled as he flipped open his wallet – a vision of mint fresh, red 20,000 lira notes. As he handed me one, he said something, giving a slow smile as Selma translated – "You will be setting the exam paper?"

Alas, no.

No sign that they have heard of Dr Norbert's disappearance.

21 June 1988

Walking from Beyazit down to the Post Office; an iron pole fell from scaffolding and landed a couple of feet ahead of me. Shouts of laughter at my near-death from building-workers high above.

Telephoned R. (Tap-tap-tap-tap-tap and you're on the international line, a jungle of metallic echoes, crossed lines and foreign tongues; tap-tap-tap-tap-tap and you're in Dublin.) My manuscript arrived safely. I said I was looking forward to getting home myself. R. – voice sounding around-the-corner clear, yet infinitely remote: "Are you?"

22 June 1988

What would we have done without Dr Norbert all year? Only now I realise how many empty hours we filled discussing him: where he was from, where each of us had seen his advertisement, what clothes he had worn at the interview? (lay in London, clerical in Dublin ...) He was what the weather would be at home – a topic of dramatic variety; never more so than this evening at our end of term party.

The Turkish teachers chose the restaurant, high up in some house down a side-street of Istiklal Caddesi. As the iron trellis gate of the old lift opened and we all appeared in the corridor, the waiters' eyes brightened – until Ceyun spoke in Turkish. No easy pickings here. They left us to one old man with an arthritic hand crooked open, as if frozen in the act of taking a tip. The tables were inspected; none would do. Three of them were moved together by a window looking across the city. The old waiter looked wistfully across the room as a party of English businessmen arrived and the others swooped like falcons.

Everyone had their own picture of Norbert in the way everyone had their own picture of this city. He told Tom that his father used to beat him. Séamus, who turned up – in a new, light, white suit – claimed he had made a pass at him. According to Deirdre, he had taken a vow of celibacy when he was twenty-one. Gail revealed that he had visited her one night and, crying, said he was lonely. (What does it say about myself that he told me he had four – Irish, English, Australian, Costa Rican – passports?)

He was a confusion, a mess: devious, generous, cruel, spontaneous, affected; so busy keeping in with everyone, a step ahead of everyone, that he didn't know who he was himself. This city had seen his kind before, a thousand, two thousand years before, I thought drunken-elegiacal as the wine went around and I looked across the evening skyline of flat Byzantine domes and onion-shaped Islamic ones: layer on layer – Greek, Roman, Jewish, Christian, Turkish. What was it to Byzantium-Constantinople-Istanbul if Norbert C. Hopkins moved on with his snail-shell of plastic junk?

But no – yet again he was a step ahead – Inci leaned forward, explaining that a friend of hers on the island said the police had been to his house. Its front door had been left ajar. Everything had been left behind: the Postman Pat and Lord Mountbatten videos; the Mona Lisa and the portrait of Pope John Paul; Shakespeare and *Confessions of a Window Cleaner*. " ... Even his – how do you say 'rahib'?"

"Priest." (Irene)

"Even his priest's clothes were there. Only his passport

and cat were missing."

"And the money."

The figure rose in auction-room jumps as the evening went on. Some parents had contributed more, so that their children should have the best in the English promised land. £40,000. The school also had donated. £50,000. So had the shrewd mayor of Istanbul. £60,000 ... His motives changed. He had been planning this for years: one big killing. No, that bossy new English teacher – "a flag-*wagger*", as Edmund called him – had discovered a drawer full of Norbert's forged degrees ("University of Bognor Regis"), so he had fled. No, it was all getting too much for him – the teachers' complaints about pay, inflation. Someone said he had been suffering from "internal bleeding"; someone else hinted at suicide ("I've played my hand"). No, he had just got bored and drifted off ...

I pictured him with cat and handbag lightfooted in another city. Where? London? Rome? New York? No ... somewhere deeper into the Mediterranean – Sicily, Tunis, Cairo – where English was a commodity like olive oil or blue denim. Already probably he was gathering another cast of characters like this about him: another spoilt priest doing penance in the brothel; another drunk obsessed by his father; another unsuccessful writer. Already probably he was in another bungalow with tapes, paperbacks and Nescafé. And another white rabbit? That seemed very important suddenly, as the wine went around again.

A violin player was moving from table to table, giving up as the noise rose. Another party was warming up, young Turkish couples out for the night. One of the women sprang up and, kicking off her shoes, skipped onto the table top. Her husband moved a dessert dish aside, took her glasses, tucked them behind his breast pocket handkerchief. She drew her blouse ends out of her skirt, tied them in a knot about her and began to dance, honey-coloured belly moving in circles with her hips to the beat of clapping hands. Arm linking Murat's, Irene was somehow clapping too. Through the open window behind, neon advertisements and minaret lights appeared and disappeared as the dancing hips swayed from side to side. One of the waiters began to dance, rising on his toes, arms outspread as if he was about to fly out the window. One-handed, Murat ate the last of his baked fish, lit a cigarette, grinned. Tom – with Stephanie again (how? why? I no longer ask) – was leaning across the table to Séamus, having a deep conversation about Israel. Murat put his cigarette between the bared white teeth of the fish and, slipping from Irene's arm, began to dance, arms outspread, on tiptoes, fingers clicking.

Leaving, everyone danced out into the corridor, dancing with the waiters while we waited for the lift. The young housewife and her party danced between the iron trellis gates and slid down out of sight. Murat danced as he waited; the lift returned (I half expected to see Norbert pop out) and when we all descended to the hall there was a cheer of welcome from the young Turkish couples, dancing now with a sleepy porter.

"OK. Where we go?" Murat said, dancing out into the street before a taxi.

We went to some nightclub in Taksim. A moment's breath in the warm night air, then we were down the inevitable basement stairs into furnace heat; the dance floor of hammered copper suggesting a foundry, and the hammer-on-anvil music and the strobe light, suggesting acetylene. Shirts open to the waist, blouses open to the breast, chests and breasts sheeted with sweat. Turk, Arab, German, French ... all speaking English. English words flying like sparks. Gold medallions, crosses, crescents and six point stars hopping on neck chains, jerking to the beat of Abba's "*Waterloo-oo*". The drinks were huge. Leaning against the bar, his back to the dancing crowd, Tom continued his conversation with Séamus, bawling into his ear that Ibrahim was the Turkish for Abraham. (Séamus: "I see!")

Deirdre, Gail, swaying from side to side, humming *The Tennessee Waltz*.

As Michael Jackson's voice filled the foundry – "*The way you make me feel* … !" – Irene took Murat's hand and led him onto the copper floor, her teak tights phosphorescent in the glare. Madonna – "*I hear your voice* … " and I danced with Inci, until her head rested on my shoulder, when an attendant approached, tapped her severely on the arm.

Afterwards I offered to see her home. (Songul, whose family enforces the curfew for women, had left the restaurant at nightfall.) Silently we went up the stairs into the dark, the air like a cold plunge, yet not sobering; warm again, walking the unlighted streets arm in arm to her apartment. A car alarm went off, shrieking like an exotic bird as I kissed her goodnight. She drew back in shock, looking up at the black windows all around, whispering suddenly from the door – "I will leave open. Come back in quarter of an hour … "

And I had been so careful, I thought as warm, trembling legs carried me about the block; sat in every night, finished my novel, posted it home. A policeman came around the corner blowing his whistle. From the next street came the lonely answering note.

The hall door was ajar, the grim cement steps lit by a twenty watt bulb; fridges and cupboards overflowed from each flat out into the landing; rows of shoes outside each door. A line of light showed beside Inci's high heels, then her hand appeared drawing me inside. She shut the door as if a stick of dynamite was balanced on the handle. As it clicked shut, she froze, pressed finger to lips, looking up listening at the ceiling, then down at the floor. I lip-read rather than heard her whisper: "You do not understand Turkish thinking." She drew a finger across her throat. I kissed her throat.

A blur of memories: skin the colour of terracotta in the night-light; a gold tooth shining in the dark; body smooth of hair, so it felt like a new, third sex. Above, below, before, behind. Ecstasy.

24 June 1988

Awkward sidelong glances from the children as I arrived in school this morning. They stood aside as I went up the steps. *They know*, I thought in panic through my hangover. I had forgotten: the exams begin today.

Olive hands behind back, big blue-stoned American fraternity ring flashing, old tan officer's shoes creaking, the headmaster went slowly up on the stage, tapped the mike and delivered a ringing speech. About school fees, so far as I could follow. The shanty town children hung on the playground railings, open-mouthed; passing gypsies reined up their horses; old folk slogging through the dust clouds stood still as six figure sums echoed from the loudspeakers outside. Another speech then, like a funeral oration, about the exams. One of the children began to cry. Through the windows I could see parents walking up and down the playground smoking cigarettes, their faces tense white as the children's. The headmaster stopped talking as Serdar Bey led in a detail of porters carrying big brown envelopes sealed with tomato-sized blobs of wax. The teachers were called up to witness the opening. Crackle in the silence. The papers were handed out. Crash as a child fainted and fell off his chair. Serdar Bey sprang down to examine the glass of water carried in. The tannoy broadcast the nine o'clock bell and the hall filled with the noise of pens. Cem wrote the single word ENGLISH at the head of his paper, then sat, goggle-eyed, looking at the dazzle-white blank below. Through my pounding headache, keeping time to its beat, Inci's words this morning as I searched my pockets for taxi money went up and down in my head – "You have not English passport?" – and she glanced at my green one.

25 June 1988

All day exam-marking. Exhausted. Selma passed.

Geoffrey's wife has organised an English-speaking social club: The Corona Ladies Circle. He's staying on next year.

Official inspection of our apartments. Edmund's cigarette-burned table ("Fair wear and *tear*") cost him a 20,000 lira fine. He dumped some old books he had bought here out in the corridor with his rubbish bags. I took one of them, Procopius's *Secret History*, to bed and read myself to sleep. How the days shape themselves about us ...

" ... At this point, I think, it would be well to describe Justinian's personal appearance. In build he was neither tall nor unusually short, but of normal height, not at all skinny but rather plump, with a round face that was not unattractive: it retained its healthy colour even after a two-day fast. To describe his general appearance in a word, he bore a strong resemblance to Domitian, Vespasian's son, whose monstrous behaviour left such a mark upon the Romans that even when they had carved up his whole body they did not feel that they had exhausted their indignation against him: the Senate passed a decree that not even the name of this emperor should remain in inscriptions, nor any statue or portrait of him be preserved. Certainly from the inscriptions everywhere in Rome, and wherever else his

144

name had been inscribed, it was chiselled out, as can still be seen, leaving all the rest intact; and nowhere in the Roman Empire is there a single likeness of him except for a solitary bronze statue, which survived in the following way.

"Domitian's consort was a woman of good birth, and highly respected, who had herself never done the least wrong to any man alive, or approved a single one of her husband's actions. So she was very highly esteemed, and the Senate at this time sent for her and invited her to ask for anything she liked. She made only one request – that she might take Domitian's body and bury it, and set up a bronze statue of him in a place of her own choosing. The Senate agreed to this; and the widow, wishing to leave to later generations a monument to the inhumanity of those who had carved up her husband, devised the following plan. Having collected Domitian's flesh, she put the pieces together carefully and fitted them to each other; then she stitched the whole body together and showed it to the sculptors, asking them to make a bronze statue portraying the tragic end of the dead man. The artists produced the statue without loss of time; and the widow took it and erected it in the street that leads up to the Capitol, on the right hand side as you go there from the Forum: it showed the appearance and the tragic end of Domitian, and does so to this day (559 AD). It seems probable that Justinian's general build, his actual expression, and all the characteristic details of his visage are clearly portrayed in this statue … "

26 June 1988

Goodbyes all round. A double handshake from Edmund. Salih ran down the supermarket steps to give me a present for my journey – a hand of bananas.

Levelling out now, thirty thousand feet up, and Istanbul has fallen behind, disappeared underneath cloud. Another year's "experience" under my belt, another thousand impressions received.

Back down there, the muezzin is calling from a myriad minarets; from Sinan's grand towers in Istanbul and Edirne, and from the whitewashed village ones, those pale strokes you see across the seas of maize. The joggers are jogging between the tower blocks. Up in one of them by now, I'd say, Séamus is doing "Everything …!" The wild dog packs are prowling in the cemeteries. By now, Edmund is on the bus to Armenia, saying to someone else, "On the map it looks like the end of the *world*." In the Greek and Armenian churches the curtains are rattling across, shutting off the priest for the Consecration. The fishermen bobbing in the brazier boats along the quays are – chop slit slip flip – making fried fish sandwiches. The gypsies are out scavenging …

Up here, looking out the window at the transparent blue sky so infinitely empty and without landmark, we seem to be hanging motionless. That's another reason I hate flying. Besides frightening the life out of me, because it frightens the life out of me, it reminds me that there is another country, another element waiting to be explored; and I feel in my bones that this other country is surrounded by walls and fences, like Metris prison, like Istanbul airport, like Omer's family summer house, like so much of Turkey.

Click! as the sign to unfasten seat belts lights up. Click! Click! And I'm even more frightened now. What is this empty, infinite space?

Whatever it is, it's something we all have in common. It's inside us and about us all. In fact, it's really the only thing we all have in common. It's there all the experiences end up, the thousand impressions drop – like the pebbles Aesop's thirsty crow dropped in the well until the water

146

brimmed over. Real pebbles and false ones: drunkenness, adultery, kindnesses, conversations, bottles of wine, laughter – they all end up in the well, where the false ones – the bits of clay or dung the crow mistook for pebbles or just dropped in anyhow – dissolve, muddy the water, don't bring that element any closer ...

Hold on! Doesn't this sound suspiciously like our old friend, Irish Catholicism? That's a real world down there. Those escaped prisoners still on the run really are still on the run, really are making their way by fields and back roads, on false papers, by night, towards the border. By now, probably, Deirdre really is on a Hilton bar high stool, swinging a plump brown leg, imitating Irene teach Murat the Conditional Mood – "If we were to put my pay and your pay together, we *would* be able to get married ... " Our coach really did kill that young man on the road to Greece. Dr Norbert really is somewhere else now. How can you say all that happened for some other airy reason?

And is that all there is – the accidental, the incidental, all that's in this past year's diary – in fact? What of that infinite, empty, clear, complete blue inches away outside this window? Why does it make me tingle with longing, excitement, as I used to when I looked in an atlas at countries waiting to be explored? Why does it make me tingle with fright too? For looking at it, I feel suddenly I would rather be like Dr Norbert, grab the lot, hold onto the pebbles, and run. And run. For what would happen to me out there, in there? Say I was as single-minded as those prisoners tunnelling out of Metris, as Inci's young man who made a way with stones across the sea to the King's daughter? Say I did drop the right pebbles until the well rose, drank the water, flew away then into that element – what would be left of *me*? Say there was someone, something out there, in there, like the Custom's Man at Istanbul airport (I thought I was going to faint when he laid a hand on my heart to test me) searching for scraps carried over from the old world? That coin in my pocket – *Herakles Soter* – that I bought from Ibrahim in Iznik, and the old Roman lamp, even that beautiful, ethereally characterless terracotta head I've hidden in my handkerchief, would they all have to go – how much more would have to go – if I were to enter that ethereally characterless world?

The power of this Toros jet. Though we seem to be at a standstill, I can feel it sending shivers down the fuselage, each touch on the stick telling me we are being carried along, silently, at awful speed. It lifts something inside me up, up intoxicatingly high. I'm travelling again. Home.

Enough writing for now. The hostess is calling us to attention, pointing out the exits, pressing an oxygen mask to her face.